TABLE OF CONTENTS

Worship Blueprints

ACKNOWLEDGMENTS

Many thanks to the following people, who help to create amazing worship experiences in their churches each week, for their wonderful contributions to this book.

Bill Carroll, the music director at Community Christian Church in Naperville, Illinois, and members of that church's teaching team: Tim Sutherland, Dave Ferguson, and John Ferguson

Rachael Cook, the experience designer at Westwinds Community Church in Jackson, Michigan

Paul Woods, the executive pastor at Sturgis Missionary Church in Sturgis, Michigan

Shane Yancey, the youth pastor at Calvary Baptist Church in Eufaula, Alabama

INTRODUCTION

Experiential Worship

If you've opened this book, you probably are at least intrigued by the idea of experiential worship. You may be an enthusiastic advocate of this form of worship and are just looking for new ideas. That's great! Jump in and use whatever you think will work in your setting.

However, you may be uncertain of what experiential worship is. So first, a definition (keep in mind that this is *a* definition, not necessarily an authoritative one): Experiential worship engages people in some type of experience that makes them think or evokes an emotion and leads them to consider how God might want to work in their lives. Obviously, the word *experience* is key in this definition. An experience engages people through a variety of senses. An experience can be surprising; in fact, it can shock people into a response.

In the past, the church has worked hard to avoid surprises and shocks in worship. We've tried not to ruffle feathers and have made our services predictable so as to avoid any discomfort on the part of pew sitters. We have rationally explained the gospel message, and many have responded in faith. A rational exposition of Scripture is not a bad thing!

However, our world has changed. To most people, *predictable* means boring, ineffective, a waste of time. People in our culture value adventure. Mystery is the opposite of predictable and, therefore, is intriguing. People coming to church today are more interested in the mystery of our faith than people have been for perhaps hundreds of years. They're more interested in experiencing something of God than hearing a logical three-point sermon with two illustrations and an application at the end. They're likely to get more out of a five-minute experience that connects them with God than from a 45-minute sermon.

Experiential worship connects people with God in ways that sermons alone can't. It draws people in and creates an opportunity for God to work within their hearts and minds. It creates starting points that can lead to conversations that further people on their journeys toward or with God. It's a tool God is using to reach people for his kingdom in our world today.

Within the pages of *Engaging Worship* are complete worship plans for experiential worship services. Use these plans however you want. If you feel that a worship plan will fit your community and your purpose as written, feel free to use it that way. More likely, you'll find a worship plan that you'd like to adapt to better fit your church. Adapt away! Just don't omit all the experiential parts because you think they're too hard or too risky. The experiences are the elements that will help your service connect with more people than ever before.

If you've never done anything very experiential in your church, enter into this form of worship with enthusiasm, and expect people to respond positively. Your attitude, demeanor, and level of enthusiasm will have a big impact on how well your people accept something different.

Give God a chance to work through experiential worship in your church. You may be surprised by the results!

How to Use This Book

Adapt the blueprints to your setting. The Worship Blueprints in *Engaging Worship* are designed to be adapted to a wide variety of settings and will work in churches of any size. In each experience we've included step-by-step instructions for creating an environment for worship as well as ideas for maximizing each experience by going all out with props, set designs, lighting, and music. You can elaborate on our ideas or pare them down. It's up to you!

The blueprints also appeal to a wide range of teaching and planning styles. Some are quite detailed and include scripts and messages that can be used verbatim, while others offer broad brushstrokes for message preparation and worship-service planning. We're confident that you'll find an approach that appeals to you in these pages.

Use the accompanying CD-ROM to augment the Worship Blueprints. The CD-ROM provides tools that will help you prepare as well as execute the worship plans in this book. For example, we've provided scripts, invitations, instructions, and commitment cards that you can download and print for all the people who will be helping to prepare your worship services. To help in the execution, we've provided videos, colorful graphics, PowerPoint presentations, and lyrics to songs that are in the public domain. We've also provided sound effects that can be played on a CD player or a boombox. You may also play them from your computer if you have software that allows you to play music CDs.

Look for this icon in the book to show you the points at which the CD-ROM intersects with the text.

Because types of media equipment and technology vary so widely among churches, we've made each component of the CD-ROM as adaptable as possible to different church settings. For example, our PowerPoint presentations are offered in two formats: One is intended for churches with Visual Projection Units (VPUs) that can project PowerPoint presentations; the other is offered as a series of individual, text-only slides that can be downloaded and printed on transparencies for projection through an overhead projector.

In addition, we've provided text files (RTF) of lyrics in the public domain so you can manipulate those files for use in your own PowerPoint or Media Shout presentations or simply download and print them for projection through an overhead projector.

All the text components of the CD-ROM may be downloaded and photocopied for local church use.

Be sure to read the "Read Me" file on the CD-ROM to facilitate your use of this product with your church's electronic equipment. If you have questions on the technical aspect of any item on the CD-ROM, please feel free to contact Group's technical support staff by calling 1-800-635-0404, extension 4414, Monday through Friday between 8 a.m. and 5 p.m. Mountain Time.

Don't forget licensing requirements. In several Worship Blueprints, we suggest that you show short clips from popular movies. In general, federal copyright laws do not allow you to use videos or DVDs (even ones you own) for any purpose other than home viewing. Though some exceptions allow for the use of short segments of copyrighted material for educational purposes, it's best to be on the safe side. Your church can obtain a license from Christian Video Licensing for a small fee. Just visit www.cvli.org or call 1-888-302-6020 for more information. When using a movie that is not covered by the license, we recommend directly contacting the movie studio to seek permission to use the clip.

In addition, most of the songs that are not in the public domain that we suggest using in these Worship Blueprints are covered by Christian Copyright Licensing International (CCLI). If your church does not currently have a license with CCLI, take a look at this organization's Web site, www.ccli.com, to find out how to obtain one.

Rehearse! After you've decided on a Worship Blueprint and adapted it to your church's unique setting, be sure to provide your technical team with instructions outlining technical cues for lighting, sound, projected images, and video changes. This will prevent miscues and unintended pauses that disrupt the emotional flow of the service and make it difficult for people to fully engage in worship.

We're excited by the possibilities inherent in experiential worship services, and we pray that these Worship Blueprints will help people open their hearts to God and grow closer to him.

Worship Blueprint 1

The Spirit Comes

Theme

Exploring the story of the coming of the Holy Spirit, what it meant to those who witnessed it, and what it means to us today

Goal

To help people understand that the gift of the Holy Spirit comes to all those who recognize Jesus as Lord

Scripture

Acts 2

SUMMARY OF THE EXPERIENCE

Mood: agitated and then somber

Synopsis: This experience is designed to engage all the senses as the story of the coming of the Holy Spirit to the apostles is told. Congregants hear and feel wind against their faces, see what appear to be tongues of fire, and hear voices speaking different languages. As Peter's charge that the people's sins were responsible for nailing Jesus to the cross is recounted, worshippers hear a hammer striking metal and watch a cross being painted on a canvas. The audience is then invited to respond by taking part in a special Communion service.

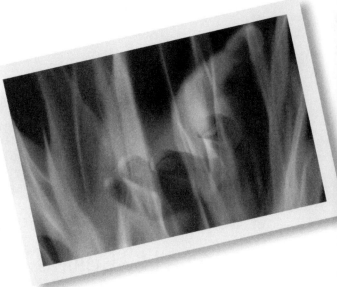

Peter replied, "Repent and be baptized, every one of you, in the name of Jesus Christ for the forgiveness of your sins. And you will receive the gift of the Holy Spirit."

—Acts 2:38

What people will

see: the semblance of fire, a cross being painted

hear: wind, an earthquake, a hammer striking metal, voices speaking in different languages, songs about the cross

feel: wind in their faces

taste: Communion elements

do: respond to the Crucifixion by taking part in Communion

CREATING AN ENVIRONMENT FOR WORSHIP

Simple Environment

At the beginning of the service, the worship area should look as it does during normal services. Special effects will be added later and will have a greater impact if the audience has no idea they're going to be used. The more black on stage initially, the better. This neutral beginning sets the tone for the story and will later act to highlight the special effects.

Place a large industrial fan out of sight of the audience, but situate it so the people will feel wind on their faces when it's turned on.

Hang a large bedsheet from the ceiling at the front of the worship area, and recruit someone from your congregation to paint a rough cross during the service and then enact shock and horror at the finished result.

Recruit a volunteer to strike a large metal hammer against a steel surface offstage.

Supplies for a Simple Environment
- industrial fan
- CD-ROM:
  Audio Track 1, "Wind and Earthquake" sound effects
  Audio Track 2, "Acts 2" sound effects
  "Blueprint 1" folder:
  - 1A, "Flames" video
  - 1B, "When I Survey the Wondrous Cross" lyrics (optional)
- person to paint a cross onstage
- bedsheet
- large paintbrush designed for exteriors
- brown paint
- purple paint
- red paint
- person to strike a hammer against a steel surface offstage
- large metal hammer
- brake drum or other solid steel surface
- Communion elements

Maximum Environment

Place a large industrial fan out of sight of the audience, but situate it so the people will feel wind on their faces when it's turned on. This experience is enhanced in a room that has lighting that is controllable and can accommodate colored gels. Create the semblance of fire by using red gel and "gobos," metal inserts that allow lights to project a certain image. In this case, combined with the red gel, the lights will produce the appearance of flames. If you don't have such lights in your worship area, you may be able to rent or borrow portable ones. In addition, gather several flame lights, and place them strategically around the worship area. (Flame lights are made of fabric that waves in an orange light, creating the effect of an open flame. They may be purchased at www.groupoutlet.com or disc jockey–supply stores or other stage-lighting outlets.) Hide the flame lights behind black boxes to increase the surprise later.

Hang a large bedsheet from the ceiling at the front of the worship area, and recruit someone from your congregation to paint a rough cross during the service and then enact horror at the finished result.

Recruit a volunteer to strike a large metal hammer against a steel surface offstage.

Additional Supplies for Maximizing the Experience
- red gels
- gobos
- flame lights

The Experience

Opening

With stage lighting at a minimum, play "Holy Visitation" by Charlie Hall or another song that conveys an ethereal feeling and invites the Holy Spirit into your worship area.

Pentecost Revisited

When the song ends, begin the special effects that are intended to re-create the sights and sounds of Pentecost. Have the band or a recording continue to play an instrumental version of the song throughout the special effects.

Start by playing Audio Track 1, the "Wind and Earthquake" sound effects. Turn up the volume and the bass of your sound system so people will feel some vibration from of the sounds.

After a minute of sound, start the industrial fan so people feel the wind as they hear the sounds of the earthquake.

1A Next, add the tongues of flame by "igniting" several different representations of fire. Start with flame lights, if you have them. Then project the "Flames" video. Last, bathe the stage and entire audience in red light if your church has that lighting capability.

In the midst of this chaos (instrumental music, wind, earthquake, and dramatic lighting), play Audio Track 2, the "Acts 2" sound effects. This track contains a cacophony of voices speaking in different languages. After about 20 seconds of chaos, the voices all begin speaking perfect English in unison. They speak Peter's words recorded in Acts 2:22-24.

After the voices subside, fade the other special effects in the opposite order in which they began, first fading the "Flames" video and red lighting, then turning off the fan, then fading the "Wind and Earthquake" sound effects until only the music is playing. Finally, end the song.

Message, Part 1

Consider using any of the following points in the first part of the message:

- Tell the story of Pentecost recorded in Acts 2, vividly describing the sights and sounds of that experience.
- These events—the wind, the fire, the languages—were so amazing that the people who experienced them wanted to know, *had* to know, what it all meant.

The Point of Culpability

At this point, have an artist enter behind the pastor and approach a large sheet hanging from the ceiling. The artist should first stare intently at the "canvas," then pick up a paintbrush, dip it in brown paint, and again stare at the canvas.

From offstage, interrupt the silence by having a hammer strike steel. (The sound of a hammer striking an automobile brake drum is resounding, but any surface made of solid iron or steel will work.) Have the sound continue, with a pause of five or six seconds between strikes.

At the sound of the hammer, have the artist react by throwing a vertical line of paint on the canvas and then resume staring at it. When the hammer strikes again, have the artist throw up another vertical line of paint. On the next strike, have the artist throw a horizontal line on the canvas. Have this process continue, first in brown, then in purple, and finally in red, as a harsh, ugly image of a cross emerges. When the pounding stops, have the artist stare in shock and horror at the image.

Then have the pastor read Acts 2:36-37a: " 'Therefore let all Israel be assured of this: God has made this Jesus, whom you crucified, both Lord and Christ.' When the people heard this, they were cut to the heart."

Then have the artist shout in despair, "What have I done?" and run, stumbling, offstage.

Message, Part 2

Consider using any of the following points in the next part of the message:

- In a way, we all were there when Jesus was crucified. The distance each of us has put between ourselves and God is what hammered Jesus to that cross.
- Jesus gave up his life to cover every one of our sins.
- God offers us salvation through the cross and the sacrifice Jesus made there.
- Communion is a time to reflect on what Jesus did for us on the cross and to confess the sins that separate us from God.
- Explain your church's expectations and procedure for partaking of Communion.

Communion

Have people come to the foot of the artist's cross to take part in Communion. During this reflective time, play any of the following songs or others of your own choosing:

1B
- "The Wonderful Cross" by Chris Tomlin
- "When I Survey the Wondrous Cross" by Isaac Watts
- "At the Cross" by Randy Butler and Terry Butler
- "Oh Lead Me" by Martin Smith
- "You Are My King" by Billy Foote
- "The Old Rugged Cross" by George Bennard

Closing

Consider using any of the following points in the last part of the message:

- Maybe you are not in a personal relationship with Jesus, and you want to know what you can do. In fact, the crowd described in Acts 2 wondered the same thing.
- Read Acts 2:37-39.
- You can repent of your sins, invite Jesus into your life, and follow him. God promises you that same power of the Holy Spirit that the new church in Acts witnessed on the day we call Pentecost.
- End with prayer.

Worship Blueprint 2

Weather the Storms

Theme

Letting Jesus calm our storms

Goal

To help people grasp that Jesus can calm the storms in their lives, just as he calmed the storm that threatened the disciples

Scriptures

Mark 4:35-41; Luke 8:22-25

SUMMARY OF THE EXPERIENCE

Mood: introspective

Synopsis: The experience begins with a movie clip from *Forrest Gump* in which Lieutenant Dan is fighting with God during a storm. At the conclusion of the clip, the song "Who Am I?" is played. The song is accentuated by movie footage of a boat in a roaring storm. Midway through the song, worshippers hear a loud clap of thunder, the lights go out, the song stops, and everyone hears the sounds of a storm at sea. When the storm subsides, a single figure clad in a wet slicker walks onto the stage carrying a lantern, the only light in the room. There he or she tells a personal story about reaching the depths of separation from God and about how God responded with hope and

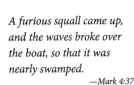

A furious squall came up,
and the waves broke over
the boat, so that it was
nearly swamped.
—*Mark 4:37*

forgiveness. At the conclusion of the story, the song resumes, accompanied by a movie clip from *The Perfect Storm* in which a boat is spared from a raging storm.

The message follows and centers on how faith can bring hope in time of crisis. It ends with a scene from *Forrest Gump* in which Lieutenant Dan resolves his differences with God.

What people will

see: images of storms, a single light in darkness

hear: sounds of a raging storm

CREATING AN ENVIRONMENT FOR WORSHIP

Simple Environment

Darken the room as much as possible, blacking out the windows with black plastic if necessary.

Recruit someone to tell a personal story about God's gift of hope and assurance during a time of fear and chaos. Make sure the person is fully capable of telling his or her story in a compelling way and can hold listeners' attention for up to 10 minutes. This story is the centerpiece of the worship experience and must be riveting.

Supplies for a Simple Environment
- *Forrest Gump* movie clips and the appropriate license for showing them (You will show two clips. For the first, cue the movie to 1:34:14, immediately after the church scene. Your sound people will have to mute the sound during one expletive that Lieutenant Dan utters while lashing out at God during the storm. End this clip at 1:35:29 after Lieutenant Dan yells for the second time, "You'll never sink this boat!" For the second clip, cue the movie to 1:37:20, immediately after Forrest shows the magazine to the lady on the park bench. End it at 1:38:04, as Lieutenant Dan swims off into the distance and Forrest says, "He never actually said so, but I think he made his peace with God.")

- CD-ROM:
  Audio Track 3, the "Storm at Sea" sound effects
  "Blueprint 2" folder:
    - 2A, "A Mighty Fortress Is Our God" lyrics (optional)
    - 2B, "All Hail the Power of Jesus' Name" lyrics (optional)
    - 2C, "It Is Well With My Soul" lyrics (optional)
- *The Perfect Storm* movie clips and the appropriate license for showing them (You will show two clips. For the first, cue the movie to 1:51:50, just after the captain says, "It's not going to let us out." End this clip at 1:53:00, after the boat is engulfed in the waves. For the second clip, cue the movie to 1:50:07, where the boat is being tossed in the waves. End it at 1:50:52, where the boat is heading toward a brightening sky.)
- person prepared to tell a personal story about how Jesus brought peace to his or her life in the midst of extreme chaos
- lantern (You can buy a battery-powered lantern at a discount store for about $7.)
- yellow rain slicker (You can buy a yellow slicker or poncho at a discount store for about $5.)
- spray bottle filled with water

Maximum Environment

This experience will be greatly enhanced if you have control of the lighting above the stage and the lighting above the audience. The effect is much more dramatic if there is no ambient light from windows. Obviously, that is not possible in all worship spaces, but if possible, use black plastic to cover all the windows.

The music is also an important element in creating the right environment. You can choose any music that fits the theme, but carefully consider the feel of the service as you consider different possibilities.

Recruit someone to tell a personal story about God's gift of hope and assurance during a time of fear and chaos. Make sure the person is fully capable of telling his or her story in a compelling way and can hold listeners' attention for up to 10 minutes. This story is the centerpiece of the worship experience and must be riveting.

THE EXPERIENCE

Song Set 1

Lead the congregation in singing any of the following songs or choose others:

- "Shout to the Lord" by Darlene Zschech
- "Trading My Sorrows" by Darrell Evans
2A • "A Mighty Fortress Is Our God" by Martin Luther
2B • "All Hail the Power of Jesus' Name" by Edward Perronet
- "Blessed Be Your Name" by Matt Redman and Beth Redman
- "I've Always Loved You" by Third Day

Forrest Gump Movie Clip 1

In this clip, Lieutenant Dan has strapped himself to the mast of a shrimping boat and wants to have it out, once and for all, with God. Play the clip.

The Perfect Storm Movie Clip 1

Play "Who Am I?" by Mark Hall. (If you don't have a band, play the song from the *Casting Crowns* CD, or play another song about calming the storms in our lives.) During the song, show the first movie clip from *The Perfect Storm* in which the boat is about to be destroyed by the wind and waves. Mute the movie so the song is the only sound people hear.

About halfway through the song, play Audio Track 3, the "Storm at Sea" sound effects. The sound effects begin with a loud clap of thunder. At that sound, turn off all the lights, have the band stop playing, and continue playing the sound effects. Listeners will hear wind, thunder, waves, and rain. If you can play the sound effects on a surround-sound system, that will make the effect much more dramatic—the louder and more powerful, the better! If a surround-sound system is not feasible, splitting the sound between front and rear speakers will add to the effect.

If possible, flash the stage lights with each thunder strike. The sounds of the storm will continue for about 90 seconds. Slowly fade the sounds of the storm, and leave people sitting in darkness.

Out of the Storm

After a few seconds, have the person who's prepared to tell his or her story walk onstage wearing a yellow slicker with the hood up and carrying a lantern—the only light in the room. (Before his or her entrance, spray the slicker with water from a spray bottle so water is dripping off the slicker as the person talks.)

Have this person walk slowly to the center of the dark stage and address the audience, beginning with the chaotic part of his or her story. Have the person keep the hood of the slicker up to add to the impression of being in the depths of darkness.

When the person begins to tell about encountering God, his or her demeanor should brighten. Have him or her pull the hood back, and, as the story turns, gradually raise the house lights. At the end of the story, the lighting should be nearly normal. Have the person turn off the lantern, nod to the audience, and exit the stage.

The Perfect Storm Movie Clip 2

Complete the song "Who Am I?" Show the second movie clip from *The Perfect Storm*, in which the same boat makes it through a storm safely and heads slowly toward a distant sunset.

Message

Consider using any of the following points in the message:
- Jesus came to the rescue of the disciples and showed he was more powerful than the worst storm (Mark 4:35-41; Luke 8:22-25).
- Jesus can calm the storms that rage in our lives, even the storms that threaten to destroy us.
- Jesus can bring peace to us during our storms and remove any distance we feel between ourselves and God.

Forrest Gump Movie Clip 2

Play the second movie clip from *Forrest Gump* in which God protects Lieutenant Dan during the storm at sea and then blesses Dan and Forrest with their largest haul of shrimp ever.

Song Set 2

Lead the congregation in singing any of the following songs or others of your choosing:
- "Good to Me" by Craig Musseau
- "All I Can Say" by David Crowder
- "Enough" by Louie Giglio and Chris Tomlin
- "40" by Bono (U2)
- "I Could Sing of Your Love Forever" by Martin Smith
- "I Will Overcome" by Charlie Hall
- **2C** "It Is Well With My Soul" by Horatio G. Spafford

Closing

Have your pastor wrap up the service with a challenge to trust God more fully and a prayer that God will help people do that.

Worship Blueprint 3

The Persecuted Church

Theme

Learning that Christians around the world are facing persecution

Goal

To increase people's awareness of the kind of persecution Christians face and to motivate people to pray for and support them

Scriptures

John 15:20; 2 Timothy 3:12; James 1:1-5; 1 Peter 5:8-9

SUMMARY OF THE EXPERIENCE

Mood: introspective

Synopsis: As worshippers enter a dimly lit worship space, they see 14 empty chairs on the stage. People participate in worship accompanied only by an acoustic guitar. After the singing, the message focuses on the fact that people are still suffering for the sake of Christ today, and the listeners are challenged to respond.

People are asked to consider the persecution Jesus suffered for their salvation as they take part in Communion.

Near the end of the service, the pastor calls 14 people by name from the crowd and asks them to sit in the chairs. Then the

pastor explains that during the last hour of the service, 14 people in the world have died for their faith in Christ.

The service concludes with worship songs and a concluding challenge and prayer by the pastor.

What people will

see: a darkened worship area lit by candles, 14 empty chairs, 14 people representing Christians who have died for their faith

hear: acoustic music

taste: Communion elements

do: sing worship songs, take part in Communion

CREATING AN ENVIRONMENT FOR WORSHIP

Simple Environment

Use as little of your normal lighting as possible, depending on candles for most of the light. Set up for Communion in whatever way you normally do. Set 14 chairs in a row on the stage.

Supplies for a Simple Environment

- 14 chairs
- candles
- worship leader playing an acoustic guitar
- Communion elements

Maximum Environment

Create the impression that the worship area is in a hidden, secretive place. Arrange potted trees in the foyer to disguise the main entrance to the worship area. Set them up so people have to walk around them in order to enter. Hang a heavy, dark curtain over the doorway so people have to push it aside. Place a small sign at the entrance that says, "You are now entering a gathering of the persecuted church."

Create song sheets with handwritten words. Make the song sheets look well worn. Distribute them at the beginning of the service, and collect them at the end.

Darken the worship area as much as possible. (This may necessitate taping black plastic over windows.) If possible, arrange seating around the middle of the room, and have the pastor speak from the center. You could even remove most of the seating and have people who are able sit on the floor.

Use candles to provide most of the lighting. You may need to add a few torch-type lamps near Communion stations. You might also direct a single spotlight on the person leading worship. The person leading worship should use an acoustic guitar only, with no amplification if feasible. Also, your pastor should use no amplification if at all feasible.

Place 14 empty chairs in a row across the stage. Set up stations around your worship area where people can partake of Communion. Arrange a candle and Communion elements on a table at each station. You'll want to have a station for about every 50 people in your congregation.

Additional Supplies for Maximizing the Experience
- potted trees
- heavy, dark curtain
- sign saying, "You are now entering a gathering of the persecuted church"
- handwritten, tattered song sheets
- Communion station for every 50 participants

The Experience

Introduction

To contribute to a somber, somewhat secretive atmosphere, don't have music playing as people arrive. The quiet and darkness will discourage talking. When it's time to begin, have your pastor introduce the topic and explain why the worship area is set up differently.

Song Set 1

Have a worship leader use only an acoustic guitar to lead the congregation in singing as many of the following songs as you wish:
- "Here I Am to Worship" by Tim Hughes
- "Trading My Sorrows" by Darrell Evans
- "Better Is One Day" by Matt Redman
- "With My Whole Heart" by Jeff E. Coleman
- "Your Love Is Deep" by Jami Smith, Dan Collins, and Susanne Bussey

Persecution Statistics

Have the pastor share the following statistics, or find more current ones at www.opendoorsusa.com or www.persecution.com.
- Nearly 100 million Christians were martyred in the 20th century.
- More people were martyred for their faith in Jesus Christ in the 20th century than in all the previous 19 combined.
- It has been estimated that 130,000 to 170,000 people die every year as a result of violence against Christianity. That means that more than 2,500 die every week, more than 357 every day, more than 14 every hour!

Message, Part 1

Consider using any of the following points in this part of the message:
- Persecution against Christians is a reality today.

- Persecution is described frequently in the Bible (Shadrach, Meshach, Abednego, Stephen, and Paul, for example).
- In 2 Timothy 3:12, Paul predicted that Christ followers would be persecuted.
- According to James 1:1-5, persecution strengthens Christians.
- Jesus suffered the ultimate persecution. The sinless God-man was crucified to provide forgiveness for our sins.

Communion

Explain your church's position on Communion. As people partake of the Lord's Supper, play reflective music.

14 Dead

After people have finished taking Communion, have your pastor call 14 people forward to sit in the chairs on the platform. The pastor should call them by name, choosing a variety of ages: mothers, fathers, grandparents, teenagers, and older children. (Because of the seriousness of this activity, don't choose younger children or youth who might make light of what's happening.)

When all 14 are seated, have your pastor explain that in the last hour, 14 Christians somewhere in the world died for their faith. These were real people, not just statistics. They were mothers, fathers, grandparents, and children. They had names and faces and were known by their friends, just like the people sitting on the stage. How should this affect the way we think and act?

Message, Part 2

Have the 14 people remain seated on the stage for the brief remaining portion of the message. If you are singing more than one song during the final song set, have the people return to their seats during the singing.

Consider using all of the following points in the next part of the message:

- We must guard against Satan's attacks (1 Peter 5:8).
- We must pray for those facing persecution.
- We must take advantage of the freedom we have to tell others about Jesus.
- We must honestly ask ourselves if we have a faith that will stand up under persecution.

Song Set 2

Choose as many of the following songs, or others of your own choosing, as you wish:

- "Take My Life" by Scott Underwood
- "Open the Eyes of My Heart" by Paul Baloche
- "One Thing" by Charlie Hall
- "Enough" by Chris Tomlin and Louie Giglio
- "Surrender" by Marc James

Closing Challenge

Challenge listeners with these questions and ideas:

- How much does your faith matter to you? Start living as if it matters.
- How much are you willing to give up for your faith? Start living as if it matters.
- Jim Elliot, who was martyred for his faith, once wrote, "He is no fool who gives up what he cannot keep to gain that which he cannot lose."

Close with prayer. Invite people to pray at the altar if they feel led to do so as your band or a CD plays reflective music.

Worship Blueprint 4

"He Has Removed Our Transgressions"

Theme

Learning to accept forgiveness

Goal

To help people realize that when God forgives their sins, he removes those stains forever

Scripture

Psalm 103:11-12

SUMMARY OF THE EXPERIENCE

Mood: festive

Synopsis: As the service opens, people will see images of animals and plants coming to life. Then a voice-over will ask questions about forgiveness. After a time of worship, video images of early attempts at flight will be projected on the screen, prompting people to consider their own attempts to overcome sin.

The pastor will discuss forgiveness and will ask everyone to complete this sentence on a card: "It would be a miracle if God could take away _____." A person on stage will read several of the cards aloud. Finally, participants will see images of helium balloons being released into the open air.

As far as the east is from the west, so far has he removed our transgressions from us.

—Psalm 103:12

What people will

see: images of animals and plants coming to life, flight, and balloons floating away

do: complete a "miracle card"

CREATING AN ENVIRONMENT FOR WORSHIP

Simple Environment

Light the worship area so it feels bright and exciting. Decorate the room with images of butterflies and balloons. Display the word *forgiven* prominently in several places. Choose upbeat, uplifting music.

End the service by projecting the CD-ROM's "Balloon Release" video or by having everyone go outside together to watch as balloons are released.

Supplies for a Simple Environment

- CD-ROM:
  "Blueprint 4" folder:
  - 4A, "Coming to Life" video
  - 4B, "Early Attempts at Flight" video
  - 4C, "Balloon Release" video
  - 4D, "Revive Us Again" lyrics (optional)

- cards that read, "It would be a miracle if God could take away_____." (Each card must have a hole punched in the upper right-hand corner, and there should be enough cards for each participant to have one.)
- helium balloons, inflated and tied to strings
- images of balloons and butterflies
- several signs that say, "forgiven"

Maximum Environment

Light the worship area so it feels bright and exciting. Decorate the room with images of butterflies and balloons. Display the word *forgiven* prominently in several places. Choose upbeat, uplifting music.

Arrange for a videographer to film someone taking the helium balloons (with the miracle cards attached to their strings) through the building and up onto the roof (using either a ladder or interior stairs). As the event is fed live onto a screen in the worship area, have the person with the balloons release them into the air. Instruct the videographer to focus on the balloons until they disappear into the distance. (The live feed is accomplished with a long video cord that runs to a video input or a video-mixing station. You might want to use two different cameras, one inside the building and one on the roof. This will prevent worry about carrying cameras up ladders, getting cords tangled, and so on.)

Additional Supplies for Maximizing the Experience
- videographer
- video equipment
- volunteer to climb onto the church roof and release balloons

THE EXPERIENCE

New Life

Have ushers distribute "miracle cards" as people enter the worship area.

4A Play the "Coming to Life" video, which portrays various plants and animals coming to life. During this video, use a voice-over to ask questions such as "Did Jesus rise from the dead?" "Can God forgive *all* my sins?" and "Why does God love me?"

Song Set 1

Select upbeat songs that tie in with the theme, such as any of these:

- "Let Everything That Has Breath" by Matt Redman
- "Beautiful One" by Tim Hughes
- "Trading My Sorrows" by Darrell Evans
- "Famous One" by Chris Tomlin and Jesse Reeves
- "Not to Us" by Jesse Reeves and Chris Tomlin
- "I Can Only Imagine" by Bart Millard

"Early Attempts at Flight" video

4B "Show the "Early Attempts at Flight" video.

Message

Consider using any of the following points in the message:
- Our attempts to overcome sin by ourselves are like these early attempts at flight—well-intentioned failures.
- God has a plan for giving us a new birth in Christ.
- If we confess our sins, God will forgive them *all* (1 John 1:9).
- God will not only forgive our sins but also remove our transgressions from us (Psalm 103:12).
- The miracle cards are intended to help us identify whatever sin, barrier, or situation in life that seems impossible to get rid of—whatever is creating distance between us and God.

Giving Them to Jesus

Ask people to fill out the miracle cards, anonymously, explaining that the cards will be collected and some will be read aloud. Have ushers collect them and take them to the front of the worship area. Read several of the cards aloud, but be sure not to read any details that would identify a particular person. As some of the cards are being read, have ushers tie the remainder of the cards together and then tie them to a bunch of helium balloons. After reading some of the cards, explain the symbolism of attaching the cards to helium balloons and releasing them to float away.

"Balloon Release" Video

4C Show the "Balloon Release" video.

Song Set 2

Sing a few more songs of your choosing, such as any of the following:
- "Jesus, Lover of My Soul" by Daniel Grul, John Ezzy, and Steve McPherson
- "Make a Joyful Noise" by Terry Butler

- "Shout to the Lord" by Darlene Zschech
- "Sing to the King" by Billy Foote
- "Your Love Oh Lord" by Brad Avery, David Carr, Johnny Mac Powell, Mark D. Lee, and Tai Anderson

 - "Revive Us Again" by William P. Mackay

Closing

Close with a brief conclusion and a prayer. Then, if you choose, lead the entire congregation outside to take part in releasing the balloons to the open air.

Worship Blueprint 5

Good 'n' Plenty

Theme

Becoming more generous with our time, our money, and our skills

Goal

To create an environment that cultivates a generous spirit

Scripture

Luke 21:1-4

SUMMARY OF THE EXPERIENCE

Mood: celebratory

Synopsis: In this service, two interactive experiences help promote a generous spirit. In the first, people are invited to fill out a commitment card and bring it to the altar as a gift to God. In the second, after having gathered change in individual containers at home for three weeks, people pour the contents into a larger container during the service. All the money is then given to a local organization that assists the community. This can be a moving experience as people hear and see the power of corporate giving.

*All these people gave their
gifts out of their wealth; but
she out of her poverty put
in all she had to live on.*
—Luke 21:4

What people will

    see: an altar and a container for gifts to God

    hear: coins dropping into a metal or wooden container

    do: complete and present a commitment card, pour change into a
    large container

CREATING AN ENVIRONMENT FOR WORSHIP

Simple Environment

Ask people to collect change in containers they supply. Use an
existing altar, or, if your worship area doesn't have an altar, set
up a long table, cover it with fabric, and place candles on it. To
collect all the change during the service, use a large container
you have on hand or can purchase inexpensively. A metal
garbage can works well because it's sturdy and the sound of the
coins being poured into it adds greatly to the overall experience.
In any case, make sure the container is sturdy enough to hold all
the change that will be collected.

    Recruit volunteers to distribute commitment cards during the
service.

Supplies for a Simple Environment
- altar
- volunteers to distribute commitment cards during the service
- large metal or wooden container for collecting the congregation's change
- CD-ROM:
  "Blueprint 5" folder
    - 5A, "Commitment Cards"
- card stock
- pens

Maximum Environment

Think of a container that symbolizes the organization to which the money from this worship experience will be donated. For example, you might choose baby bottles if the money will be given to an organization that helps new mothers provide for their babies. Purchase a container for everyone who will participate in the experience.

To emphasize the idea that giving is a holy, consecrated act, build an elaborate altar prior to the experience. Encourage your team's creativity in the design and construction of the altar. Here's one idea: Use a grinder to etch various names of God onto a sheet of Plexiglas. (Make the lettering large enough for people to read the names from most places in your worship area.) You might etch Hebrew names on one side and English names on the other. Then use strong wire to hang the Plexiglas. Pile cinder blocks artistically beneath the hanging Plexiglas, and place incense on the cinder blocks. Light the altar by placing some lights in the middle of the pile of cinder blocks so the lights cast a nice glow on the Plexiglas.

Recruit artistic people in your congregation to design and construct a large, sturdy container into which people will pour their change.

Because the accumulated change will be heavy, metal, wood, or another strong material should be used to build this container.

Recruit volunteers to distribute commitment cards during the service.

Additional Supplies for Maximizing the Experience
- containers for individuals to use to collect change at home
- altar built especially for this experience
- specially designed and constructed container for collecting the congregation's change

THE EXPERIENCE

Three Weeks Before the Event

Explain that the church is launching a three-week effort to gather funds for a local organization. Describe the organization's purpose and scope, and, if possible, ask someone from the church to promote the organization by describing a positive experience he or she has had with it. Ask people to deposit their pocket change in a container each night for the next three weeks, and tell them the date the money will be collected.

One to Two Weeks Before the Event

5A Copy the commitment card on page 42 (also available as a printable download on the CD-ROM, segment 5A) onto card stock. This card gives people an opportunity to commit their time, skills, energies, and treasure to serving Christ.

Opening Music

Play "Dare You to Move" by Jonathan Foreman. If you use recorded music, this song may be found on Switchfoot's *The Beautiful Letdown* album.

Song Set 1
- "Famous One" by Chris Tomlin and Jesse Reeves
- "Indescribable" by Chris Tomlin

Opening Remarks
Have the pastor introduce the idea of being a generous person and of the church being a generous community. Just as Christ has been and is generous to us each day, we should be generous Christ followers.

Message, Part 1
Consider using any of the following points in the message:
- We can use this altar to present our gifts to God, and he will smell the sweet aroma that flows up from our sacrifices.
- Even though we are broken people and our journey toward God is full of stops and starts, we can approach the altar and communicate with God. He will accept us in our broken state.
- Share personal stories of imperfect generosity. Even though we often fall short of our intentions to be generous, we are still called to become people who are characterized by a generous spirit.
- Describe specific ways for people to demonstrate their generosity, such as participating on the worship team, working in the children's program, hosting or leading a Bible study, sharing financial resources, and committing to pray for the needs of the church.
- Describe the commitment cards, and explain that they are a way to help people make their commitments more immediate and concrete. Invite people to fill out the cards, committing to be more generous with their time, skills, and resources. Explain that they may remain anonymous or, if they would like people from the church to follow up with them, they may include their names and contact information. In either case, emphasize that people are under no obligation to complete

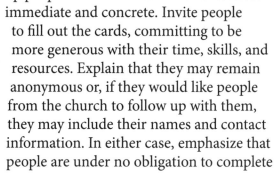

the cards. Once people have filled out their cards, invite them to take them to the altar and offer them to God.

Song Set 2

As people approach the altar and place their cards there, have the band or a recording play "Draw Me Close" by Kelly Carpenter, followed by an instrumental piece.

Message, Part 2

Consider using any of the following points in the next part of the message:

- Describe ways people have been generous to you and what their generosity has meant in your life.
- Remind listeners of the needs of the local organization that has been selected to receive the church's gift.
- Invite people to come forward and empty the change they've collected over the previous three weeks into the large container.

Have people remain silent as they approach the large container and pour their change into it. If some families collected their change together, encourage all the members of each of those families to approach the container together and pour in their coins. Allow people to do this at their own pace. If you play soft music during this time, be sure the music doesn't overpower the sound of coins being poured into the container. Allow a minute of silent reflection after the last person has poured in his or her change.

Song Set 3

Play songs that are appropriate to the theme and your setting. You might consider any of the following:
- "One Thing" by Charlie Hall
- "Breathe" by Marie Barnett
- "Our Love Is Loud" by David Crowder

Closing

Arrange for someone either from within the church or outside of it to share a dramatic story of generous giving, then conclude the service with prayer.

"As he looked up, Jesus saw the rich putting their gifts into the temple treasury. He also saw a poor widow put in two very small copper coins. 'I tell you the truth,' he said, 'this poor widow has put in more than all the others. All these people gave their gifts out of their wealth; but she out of her poverty put in all she had to live on'" (Luke 21:1-4).

Lord, help me to remember the example of this widow, who gave out of the abundance of a full and grateful heart. In remembrance of her, I commit to give
- my time in the form of regular prayer for the needs of this church
- my energies in the form of occasional or regular volunteer activity
- a certain amount of money
- a percentage of my income

to the cause of Jesus each week.

(Optional) Name _____

(Optional) E-mail address or phone number _____

- -

"As he looked up, Jesus saw the rich putting their gifts into the temple treasury. He also saw a poor widow put in two very small copper coins. 'I tell you the truth,' he said, 'this poor widow has put in more than all the others. All these people gave their gifts out of their wealth; but she out of her poverty put in all she had to live on'" (Luke 21:1-4).

Lord, help me to remember the example of this widow, who gave out of the abundance of a full and grateful heart. In remembrance of her, I commit to give
- my time in the form of regular prayer for the needs of this church
- my energies in the form of occasional or regular volunteer activity
- a certain amount of money
- a percentage of my income

(Optional) Name _____

(Optional) E-mail address or phone number _____

Worship Blueprint 6

Taste the Deep

Theme
Moving out of shallow faith into God's deeper, more freeing life

Goal
To help worshippers deepen their understanding of their own condition and of God's offer of a more abundant life

Scriptures
John 8:31-32; John 8:34-36; John 10:10; John 14:6; Galatians 5:1

SUMMARY OF THE EXPERIENCE

Mood: exciting

Synopsis: Many Christians live their lives thinking that an abundant spiritual life comes only when they get to heaven. They're too timid to step out in faith and join in God's big story *right now*. For many this may be because they don't know how it feels to truly rely on God. This worship experience is intended to open the door for God to speak to the hearts of worshippers about this amazing journey.

Worshippers will see images related to diving and will watch a humorous video about swimming in shallow water. They'll watch

I have come that they may have life, and have it to the full.

—John 10:10

a movie clip and then a live drama that culminates in a choice that worshippers must make to either continue living small lives or join God on his journey.

What people will

see and hear: images related to diving, "Braving the Deep" video, *The Lord of the Rings* movie clip, "A Bread and Water Feast" drama

taste: unflavored croutons and chocolate

CREATING AN ENVIRONMENT FOR WORSHIP

Simple Environment

Place a pool rope above the doors to the worship area. Make sure people can see it as they enter.

Make four large poster-board signs reading, "Banquet This Way," "Big Feast! Everyone Invited!" "Free Banquet," and "Banquet This Way." Place the first sign toward the back of the worship area, the second somewhere near the middle, the third near the stage, and the fourth on a table on the stage. Place a loaf of plain white bread and a bottle of water on the table.

Supplies for a Simple Environment
- *The Lord of the Rings: The Two Towers (Special Extended Edition)* movie clip and the appropriate license for showing it (Cue the first disk to 1:34:22, when Eowyn removes the sword. End it at 1:35:47 when Aragorn bows and walks away.)
- 3 actors to perform the drama "A Bread and Water Feast" (pp. 49-50) and a copy of the script for each (The script is also available as a printable download on the CD-ROM, segment 6E.)

- CD-ROM:
  "Blueprint 6" folder:
  - 6A, "Diving Deep" video
  - 6B, "Braving the Deep" video
  - 6C, "Come, Thou Fount" lyrics (optional)
  - 6D, "A Bread and Water Feast" script
- table
- loaf of white bread
- bottle of water
- poster board and markers
- plastic bags each containing 1 unflavored crouton and 1 wrapped Hershey's Kiss (You'll need one bag for each worshipper.)
- volunteers to distribute the bags

Maximum Environment

Spray paint "DIVE?" in a bright color on several old diving boards or props that look like diving boards. Place the props outside the door to the worship area. These could also be used as a focal point in the worship area. Use a pool rope (the kind with floats that separates the deep end from the shallow end) to add to the décor of your room. Hang it from the ceiling, or drape it along the stage. Use overhead projectors to project images of cliff divers onto the walls or ceiling.

Make four large poster-board signs reading, "Banquet This Way," "Big Feast! Everyone Invited!" "Free Banquet," and "Banquet This Way." Place the first sign toward the back of the worship area, the second somewhere near the middle, the third near the stage, and the fourth on a table on the stage. Place a loaf of plain white bread and a bottle of water on the table.

Additional Supplies for Maximizing the Experience
- spray paint
- old diving boards
- images of cliff divers

THE EXPERIENCE

6A Project the "Diving Deep" video onto the screen as people enter.

Song Set 1
- "Dive" by Steven Curtis Chapman
- "No One Like You" by David Crowder, Jack Parker, Jason Solley, Jeremy Bush, Mike Dodson, and Mike Hogan
- "Majesty" by Jack Hayford

"Braving the Deep" Video

6B *Play the "Braving the Deep" video. At its conclusion, have the pastor read the following text or use it as a springboard for the message.*

Pastor: That's pretty silly, isn't it? Elijah didn't really brave anything. He splashed around in shallow water, even though the real adventure wasn't there next to the shore—the real adventure was out in the rough water. The real adventure was out in the deep.

Most Christians live their lives like Elijah

James. They thrash around at the edge of Christianity and wonder why their lives don't have more meaning. Today you're invited to leave the edge of Christianity and dive into God's deep water.

You're invited to cross the rope from the shallow end of life and dive headfirst into the deep end. The God of the universe— the God who created everything, the all-powerful God—invites you to join him on a great journey. He calls you to leave behind a small life paddling around in the shallow end and dive into all that he has to offer. It is a life filled with danger and uncertainty, but it is also a life filled with wonder, amazement, fulfillment, and—most of all—true worship. Will you dive in?

Song Set 2

- "In the Secret" by Andy Park
- "Not to Us" by Jesse Reeves and Chris Tomlin
- "Better Is One Day" by Matt Redman
6C • "Come, Thou Fount" by Robert Robinson

The Lord of the Rings Movie Clip

Show the clip. Its connection to the message is that many Christians have adapted to shallow-water living and are content in spiritual "cages."

Go Deeper

Pastor: In this clip, the biggest fear was of the cage. But as Christians, many of us have reached a point where we are content in a cage. We used to have big dreams about how we would allow God to work in our lives, but we've given up on them. We've learned to go through the motions—and we like it that way! Many Christians are astonished to hear that the Christian life should be a little dangerous. They've forgotten that we aren't called to sit quietly in pews; we are called to a life of adventure. But many of us are too afraid of the deep water and too content in the shallows to really have the life that Jesus promises in John 10:10: "I have come that [you] may have life, and have it to the full."

Teaching Points

Consider using any of the following points in the next part of the message:

- Three characteristics of living in the shallows:
  1. You don't take risks for God: You don't tell others about your faith; you don't step out in faith; you don't do anything that requires you to relinquish control.
  2. You don't understand worship. You see other people getting excited, and you think it is because their personalities are different from yours. You can't think of any other reason people would respond like that. Real worship is more than just singing; it's about living life on the edge with God—that's where you see how great he is.
  3. You have a longing you can't explain. You long to be a part of God's big story, but as long as you stay in the shallow waters, you will never be spiritually fulfilled.

Pastor: Some of you here are living this way right now. You're wading in the shallow waters because you don't understand how great life is in the deep with God. It is scary, but it is wonderful.

Tell a story of something daring you have done—bungee jumping or finally leaping from a rope swing that you were afraid of when you were a child, for example.

Pastor: We've all confronted things that scare us but are worth pursuing. Think about the first time you were in love. There is nothing more frightening than opening your heart to someone, but there is also nothing more wonderful. To experience all that life is about, to experience all that God is about, you have to get out of the shallows and head into deep, sometimes dangerous waters. You have to wade in above your head and move beyond your own strength to that place where you are forced to rely on God. That's where real living begins.

Teaching Points

Consider using any of the following points in the next part of the message:

- Three things happen when you live out in the deep:
  1. You live the adventure your heart longs for.
  2. Your true self becomes your only self. You don't have to worry about people "seeing the real you" because the real you is who you show to the world.
  3. Others are drawn to you. There's something magnetic about a Christian living deeply with God.

Pastor: So you have a choice today. Will you choose to continue living a half-life in the shallows, or will you follow God into the deep?

6D "A Bread and Water Feast" Drama

Persons 1 and 2 enter from the back of the worship area and begin saying their lines as the pastor is leaving the stage. They continue toward the stage as they come across each sign. Be sure they have microphones or very loud voices because their backs are to parts of the audience as they are walking and talking. If the room is large, you may need to spotlight them so everyone can immediately pick them out of the crowd.

Person 1: I'm so hungry.

Person 2: Me, too. I feel like I haven't eaten in a week.

Person 1: I *haven't* eaten in a week.

Person 2: *(As they encounter the first sign)* Hey! What's this? "Banquet This Way."

Person 1: Wow! I wish we could go to that.

Person 2: Yeah. Me, too.

Person 1: *(As they encounter the second sign)* Look! Here's another one: "Big Feast! Everyone Invited!"

Person 2: Everyone's invited! We can go! *(Suddenly sad)* But I bet we don't have enough money.

Person 1: *Enough* money? I don't have *any* money.

Both: *(As they encounter the third sign)* "Free Banquet!" We can go! *(Sung to the old-school McDonald's jingle. If this won't resonate with your audience, choose a song from a more recent commercial)* Big Mac, Filet-o-Fish, Quarter Pounder, french fries, icy Coke, thick shakes, sundaes, and apple pies!

Person 2: *(As they approach the table)* Hey! There's some food!

Person 1: This is a feast?

Person 2: Who cares? It's food, isn't it?

Person 1: Yeah, but that sure was false advertising. Look around; maybe there's something else.

Person 2: There is nothing else, just the sign saying, "Feast This Way."

Person 1: Oh, well. At least it is food. *(They start to eat.)*

Person 3 enters from one side of the stage.

Person 3: Are you guys coming?

Person 2: Coming where?

Person 3: To the feast.

Person 1: You mean this isn't it?

Person 3: Of course not. There's all the food you could ever imagine right over here. *(Person 3 begins to walk offstage while motioning for Persons 1 and 2 to follow.)*

Person 1: *(Whispering)* I told you there was more. We should have known!

Persons 1 and 2 start to follow Person 3, but Person 2 takes the bread with him or her.

Person 3: Why are you taking that?

Person 2: I'm still hungry.

Person 3: There's a feast right over here.

Person 2: But what if there isn't?

Person 3: You just have to trust me.

Person 1: Come on, which would you rather have: a few pieces of bread or a feast?

Person 2: But I'm so hungry. If there isn't anything over there, then I'll have this bread as a backup.

Person 3: You can't take that to the feast.

Person 1: Come on; just leave it.

Person 2: I can't! I'm too hungry to trust. You guys go ahead.

Person 3 shrugs and walks offstage.

Person 1: Are you really not coming?

Person 2: I just can't risk it.

Person 1: Well, I guess I'll see you later.

Person 2: Yeah, guess so.

Person 1 walks offstage.

Person 2: *(Chews the bread for a moment and realizes that it isn't really all that good. After some obvious deliberation, he leaves the bread and runs after the others.)* Forget this bread; I want the feast!

Choosing the Feast

Immediately after the drama, have volunteers distribute small plastic bags containing Hershey's Kisses and croutons as the pastor and band (if you have one) return to the stage.

Pastor: *(Speaks as bags are being distributed)* So here is your choice: Will you choose the small life, the safe life, the life you have in your hands, or will you take a chance? Will you risk leaving that small life behind to get the larger-than-life existence that God offers you in the deep? You have in your hands a crouton and a piece of chocolate. Both of them will give you a little nourishment; both of them will work your jaw muscles and be digested by your body. But one of them isn't very interesting. The crouton, while functional, isn't very flavorful. It lacks something that chocolate can never be accused of lacking: taste. Think about the bread as that small life you know. It represents life in the shallows. On the other hand, the chocolate represents God's deep, abundant life.

Which will you choose? Are you willing to dive in? Take some time now to ask God to show you how you are living a shallow spiritual life; then make your choice: bread or chocolate, shallow or deep, your small life or God's abundant life. The choice is yours.

Play about three minutes of soft music as people pray and choose whether to eat the croutons or the chocolate.

Song Set 3

Sing a few more songs as a group. Invite people to come to the altar to pray or to respond to God's prompting. Choose songs such as the following:

- "Consuming Fire" by Tim Hughes
- "Breathe" by Marie Barnett

Pastor: As you leave today, will you choose to live a small life, or are you willing to trust God and go deeper with him?

Worship Blueprint 7

Infinitely Creative Creator

Theme
Worshipping God through the wonder of creation

Goal
To open worshippers' eyes to the wonders of God around them and increase their awareness of creation as they move through their daily lives

Scriptures
Nehemiah 9:5b-6; Psalm 8:3-4; Psalm 136:1-9; Psalm 148; Isaiah 40:26-31

SUMMARY OF THE EXPERIENCE

Mood: quiet anticipation

Synopsis: This worship gathering uses God's infinite creativity in nature as a jumping-off point for worship. Through video and guided imagery, worshippers are encouraged to focus on God's creation and ultimately on the fact that God created them. It is a time of celebration as worshippers see the glory of God all around them. It should also inspire worshippers to worship God when they consider creation after they leave the gathering.

When I consider your heavens, the work of your fingers, the moon and the stars, which you have set in place...

—*Psalm 8:3*

What people will

see: flowers and other living plants, images of creation, the intricacy and beauty of a feather

hear: Scriptures and songs celebrating God's infinite creativity, a guided prayer

smell: live flowers and plants

touch: modeling clay or modeling dough, feathers, and impressions of feathers in clay

do: make their own creations using clay, make impressions of feathers in clay, write or draw praises to God

CREATING AN ENVIRONMENT FOR WORSHIP

Simple Environment

Add live plants and potted flowers to the stage area. Create a soft ambience by lowering the lights and placing lots of candles around the room.

Supplies for a Simple Environment
- CD-ROM:
  "Blueprint 7" folder:
  - 7A, "How Great Thou Art" lyrics (optional)
  - 7B, "Creation" video

- 7C, "Great Is Thy Faithfulness" lyrics (optional)
- 7D, "Creation" guided prayer
- modeling clay or modeling dough, separated into individual portions and placed in plastic bags (You'll need enough for each worshipper to have a small portion. Before the experience, use a portion of clay to create a model of a machine, and be prepared to explain how the machine would work if it were the real thing.)
- reader for the "Creation" guided prayer (p. 58) (This prayer is also available as a printable download on the CD-ROM segment 7D.)
- feathers (You'll need enough for each worshipper to have one. Bags of feathers are available at most craft stores. Make sure the feathers have strong central shafts and vanes and are not simply fuzz.)
- paper and pens (You'll need enough for each worshipper to have one of each.)
- fresh flowers and other plants
- several volunteers to distribute clay, feathers, paper, and pens
- Scripture readers representing several generations: children, youth, adults, and senior adults

Maximum Environment

Fill the room with live plants, including lots of flowers. Use muslin as a background for painting large nature backdrops for the stage area. They don't have to be photo-realistic; they can simply imply shapes and ideas from creation. (Avoid cartoonlike nature scenes unless your primary audience is children.) Flank the doors to the worship area with two large fish tanks. Create a soft ambience by lowering the lights and placing lots of candles around the room. As people enter, project images of wildlife and nature on the screen.

Additional Supplies for Maximizing the Experience
- muslin
- paint
- artist to paint backdrops
- 2 large fish tanks
- candles
- images of wildlife and nature scenes

THE EXPERIENCE

Much of the experience consists of congregational singing followed by Scripture readings. Set up a place away from the spotlight where the readers can stand without being a distraction. The verses and songs should flow right into each other without a silence before or after the songs.

Song and Reading Set 1

7D **Song 1:** "How Great Thou Art" by Carl Boberg and Stuart K. Hine
Reading 1: Psalm 148
Song 2: "God of Wonders" by Marc Byrd and Steve Hindalong
Reading 2: Isaiah 40:26-31

My Creation

Distribute clay, paper, and pens to everyone.

Ask worshippers to use the clay to create simple machines. Explain that the machines don't have to work, but participants should be able to explain how they would work if they had enough time and the right materials to create them.

To help get them started, display your own clay machine and explain how it would work if it were the real thing.

Play music as worshippers create, and allow them to have fun with their creations. After three to five minutes have them gather in groups of four or five, and ask them to explain their creations to one another. After they've shared, have the pastor read the following or use it as a springboard for the message.

Pastor: Using the power of your imagination, you made something new and different from a formless lump of clay. It might not be pretty or perfect, but it came from a spark of creativity inside you. Some of us have more of this spark than others, but we all have a desire to create, to make something new. We all have this spark because we are created in the image of God, the infinitely creative Creator. He is the master Artist, the ultimate Imaginer. He is the great creator King. Today we will consider the awesome wonder of his creation as we worship him.

"Creation" Video

7B Play the "Creation" video.

Song and Reading Set 2

Song 1: "Indescribable" by Laura Story
Reading 1: Psalm 8:3-4
Song 2: Choose from these options:

7C
- "Great Is Thy Faithfulness" by Thomas O. Chisholm
- "My Lord Is Near Me All the Time" by Barbara Fowler Gaultney

Reading 2: Nehemiah 9:5b-6 (Begin with "Stand up and praise.")

7D "Creation" Guided Prayer

This guided prayer requires slow pacing to be effective. Each ellipsis (…) represents a significant pause. Listen to the Holy Spirit as you are speaking, and allow time for people to think of ideas. To set an appropriate mood, consider playing soft music such as a softly picked guitar during the prayer.

Reader: Close your eyes and think of a place in nature that inspires you. It could be a place you've visited often or a place you've seen only in pictures…Now imagine yourself in that place…What does it look like?…What does it smell like?…When you are quiet and still, what do you hear?…Now imagine God is right there beside you…He is pointing out the handiwork of his creation to you…showing you things he has made…What do you say to him?…

Now open your eyes and, using the pen and paper you were given earlier, compose a short poem or paragraph praising God for what you saw in your mind's eye. Describe the wonder of God's creation in detail as you praise his majesty. If you would prefer to draw, feel free to do that instead.

As soft, contemplative music plays, give everyone plenty of time to create his or her own message of praise. Then ask people to share their praises with the group at large or with smaller groups, depending on the size of your congregation.

An Impression of Praise

Distribute feathers.

Pastor: Return to your clay creations. Press them down until you've formed a flat disk. When you receive a feather, take a minute to examine it. Look at the intricacies of the vanes, and notice the variations in color. Think about the amazing creativity of God that is reflected in something as simple as a feather.

Give people a few minutes to examine their feathers.

Pastor: Now make an impression of your feather in the clay.

Give people a moment to press the feathers into the clay.

Pastor: Lightly trace the contours of the impression your feather made in the clay. Feel the ridges and valleys. Now think about your daily life. Does God's creation make an impression on you throughout the week? Do the wonders that he has placed around you enter your thoughts? God's amazing creation should be a constant source of wonder and worship. Don't let another day go by without letting it make an impression on you.

Closing

Pastor: I want to leave you with one final thought. We've thought about the wonder of God's creation; we've considered how

majestic, mighty, and creative God is; we've examined the intricacies and wonder of even the smallest details of this world. As you leave, remember that this is the same Creator who created you and that he chose you to be more than a creation, more than simply a servant. He chose you to be his child. You were created by God; you were chosen to be his child; you are a child of the King. You are the ultimate work of art. Let us praise our God, our Creator, our King, our Father. Let's worship God in all his creation.

Song Set 3

- "Creator King" by Mary MacLean

Final Words

Pastor: Now go and let God's creation make an impression on you. Take time to stop and thank God for all he has created, especially for creating you.

Worship Blueprint 8

Tabernacle Worship

Theme

Comparing the Tabernacle of the Old Testament and the worship that happened there with our lives today

Goal

To show how the Tabernacle is relevant to our relationship with God today

Scriptures

Exodus 25:8-9; Exodus 29:42-43; Exodus 30:18-21; Exodus 38:8; Hebrews 10:10

SUMMARY OF THE EXPERIENCE

Mood: quiet reflection and self-examination

Synopsis: This experience takes people on a walk through the outer courts of the Tabernacle and uses that as a model for how they are to interact with God. Participants receive an invitation to enter into fellowship with God, learn about the Tabernacle, and examine their own lives while looking at themselves in mirrors. At the conclusion of the service, people are asked if they're willing to commit to represent the Tabernacle to the world by taking the love of God with them. They're given pieces of cloth as a reminder of their commitment.

Then have them make a sanctuary for me, and I will dwell among them.
—*Exodus 25:8*

What people will

see: their own images in mirrors, their images covered by the cross

smell: incense

touch: cloth

do: view themselves in a mirror and consider their sins, think about their sins being covered by the Cross, receive a piece of cloth as a symbol of their commitment to take God to the world

CREATING AN ENVIRONMENT FOR WORSHIP

Simple Environment

8A Download "An Invitation," and print one for everyone in the congregation. Enclose each invitation in an envelope, and seal the envelopes.

Burn mild incense near the entrance to the worship area so people walk through it as they enter.

Supplies for a Simple Environment
- incense
- CD-ROM:
    "Blueprint 8" folder:
    - 8A, "An Invitation" (1 for each person)
    - 8B, PowerPoint presentation
- envelopes

- 1 small mirror for each person (These are available from Oriental Trading Company [www.orientaltrading.com] in bulk.)
- 1 small cross sticker for each person (Be sure they're small enough to fit on the mirrors.)
- volunteers to distribute the invitations, mirrors, and cross stickers
- small pieces of cloth
- counselors to pray with people at the end of the service

Maximum Environment

Drape the worship space with rough cloth, such as unbleached muslin, to evoke the sensation of being in a tent. Hang long pieces of fabric around the walls—especially framing the stage—to add to the illusion.

If you have a worship band, hang the cloth so it hides the band and prevents it from being the focal point. You might add backlighting so band members' silhouettes are visible.

For added depth, use simple slide projectors and overhead projectors to project verses or symbols of worship onto the material from the back. Burn mild incense near the entrance to the worship area so people walk through it as they enter.

Add the smells of cooking meat and baking bread to the worship area. Use a small electric grill to cook inexpensive cuts of meat throughout the service. Use a bread maker to bake bread or a toaster oven to heat up sweet-smelling bread. Place both the grill and the bread maker or toaster oven out of the way, and have someone monitor them for safety.

Additional Supplies for Maximizing the Experience
- rough cloth, such as unbleached muslin
- Scripture verses or symbols of worship projected onto backdrops
- electric grill
- meat
- bread maker and dough or toaster oven and bread

The Experience

Opening

Have the pastor read the following text or use it as a springboard for the message.

Pastor: Welcome to the Tabernacle. God instructed Moses on the design and function of the Tabernacle. It was the place where God was worshipped for generations and was the symbol of his connection with his people. As a place of worship, it wasn't a sterile, quiet place; rather, it was full of activity, beauty, and the smells of sacrifices being presented to God. It was designed to constantly remind the Israelites of the awesome wonder of their holy God. We have met here today to celebrate that wonder and to draw closer to that amazing God. Join us as we praise him.

Song Set 1

Select two upbeat songs about the greatness of God, such as these:
- "O Praise Him" by David Crowder
- "Beautiful One" by Tim Hughes
- "Majesty" by Jack Hayford
- "Great Is the Lord" by Michael W. Smith

God Initiates Contact

8B PowerPoint Slide 1: "God Initiates Contact." Have volunteers distribute invitations as the pastor begins the message, using any of the following points:
- It was God who first decided to reach out to us.
- Since the Fall people have been running away from God.
- *Read Exodus 25:8-9.* God initiated contact with us by creating his dwelling place here on earth. In the descriptions of the Tabernacle in the book of Exodus, God calls it a place where he will meet with his people.
- *Read Exodus 29:42-43.* The Tabernacle demonstrated to the world that God desired fellowship with humanity.
- Through Jesus, God opened the door for everyone to meet with him. God actually invites humanity to have fellowship with him.

At this point, have people open their invitations.

Pastor: Can you imagine? God, the infinite creator of the universe, decided to meet with you. He wants to know you intimately. He wants to dwell with you and be close to you. As we move through this time of worship, don't lose track of this important truth: God decided to meet with you. Let us seek to meet with him.

Song Set 2

Select two songs about meeting with God, such as these:
- "In the Secret" by Andy Park
- "Meet With Me" by Lamont Hiebert
- "Open the Eyes of My Heart" by Paul Baloche
- "Better Is One Day" by Matt Redman

God Provides Redemption

8B **PowerPoint Slide 2:"God Provides Redemption."** Use any of the following points in the next part of the message:

- As a person entered the Tabernacle on the way to the "Holy of Holies"—the place in which God himself dwelt—he first needed to walk past the altar.
- God is holy, and we are not. God can't have any dealings with unholy people. So God provided a way for his people to have fellowship with him: He created the sacrifice.
- In the Old Testament, God required the sacrifice of a perfect lamb. In the New Testament, God sent his Son, Jesus, to be that perfect sacrifice for us.
- *Read Hebrews 10:10.* Jesus paid the price so we could have fellowship with God, once and for all. Too often when we seek God's presence, we forget the price that was paid to give us that access.
- The Tabernacle was a constant reminder of the price paid for sin. As we continue to worship, let's focus on that sacrifice and lift up our thanks to God.

Song Set 3

Select two upbeat songs about the Cross, such as these:
- "Above All" by Lenny LeBlanc and Paul Baloche
- "Once Again" by Matt Redman
- "How Deep the Father's Love for Us" by Stuart Townend
- "You Are My King" by Billy Foote

God Restores Fellowship

8B PowerPoint Slide 3: "God Restores Fellowship." Use any of the following points in this part of the message:

- *Read Exodus 30:18-21.* As we move deeper into the Tabernacle, the next article of worship we encounter is the bronze basin used by the priests to wash their hands and feet before they entered into the presence of God. This wasn't a complete washing; the priests were already consecrated and made clean. This was a reminder for daily cleansing.
- In the same way, once we have been forgiven by Jesus, we have no need for an additional cleansing, but we do need to examine our lives and confess our sins regularly.
- The remarkable thing about the bowl in the Tabernacle was that it was made of mirrors. *Read Exodus 38:8.* (These weren't glass mirrors; they were pieces of highly polished bronze.) Each time the priests looked into the basin to wash, they would see their own reflections.

Have volunteers begin to distribute mirrors to the congregation.

- Restored fellowship with God comes through an examined heart. As you continue to walk with God, you should daily examine who you are and confess your sins to him. Confession is agreeing with God. God, through the Holy Spirit, shows us our sin, and we confess it by agreeing that we have done wrong.
- Right now, come to the basin of daily cleansing by examining yourself in your mirror. Listen as God reveals your sins to

you. Confess those sins to God, and trust in his forgiveness. *Give everyone time to speak with God. Play soft music during this time. After a few minutes, have volunteers begin distributing the cross stickers. With the music still playing softly, remind people of the sacrifice of God and the forgiveness available through the Cross.*

The Filter of the Cross

Use any of the following points in this part of the message:

- God may be revealing sins to you that you haven't dealt with in a long time.
- Some of you may look at yourselves in the mirror and think, "How could God ever forgive me?" We must never forget that when God looks at you, he sees you through the filter of the Cross.
- When you make a faith commitment to Christ, you receive a new nature, a new heart. If you have committed your life to Christ, then your sins are paid for.
- Place your sticker in the center of your mirror, and look at yourself the way God sees you—through the filter of the Cross.
- If you don't know Jesus in a personal way, consider what is holding you back from becoming a Christ follower.

Give people a few moments to place their stickers and meditate.

Pastor: Christ tore the veil that separated God from us. Jesus provided the way for us to fellowship with God. We should never lose our holy fear of God, but we must remember that we'll always be invited to worship at his feet.

Song Set 4

Select two songs about entering into God's holy presence, such as these:

- "Facedown" by Matt Redman
- "We Fall Down" by Chris Tomlin

God Invites Everyone

8B PowerPoint Slide 4: "God Invites Everyone." Use any of the following points in this part of the message:

- The Tabernacle was God's mobile presence in the world.

It wasn't set up to be stationary; it moved with his people. In the same way, God now lives in your heart. You are his mobile presence in the world. You are God's new tabernacle.

- As we have sought the face of God here in this place today, what has God spoken to you? Have you been challenged, changed? Have you worshipped him here? Worship requires more of you than simply saying words.
- Ultimately the Tabernacle was a place of sacrifice, and while Jesus paid our atoning sacrifice, we must remember that worship requires that we sacrifice as well. It requires you to do more than say words in here; it requires actions of you out there.

Pastor: We're going to close with a few songs. Let your heart cry out in praise to God, and let him speak to your heart. After you leave, will you show God to the people you meet? Will you take God with you and share his love? Will you be God's tabernacle to the world?

There are people around the room with small pieces of cloth. If you will commit to take the presence of God with you as you leave this place, then go to them. They will give you a piece of cloth to remind you that you are God's tabernacle in the wilderness of life. And if you'd like them to, they'll pray with you.

Song Set 5

Select songs such as these:
- "Consuming Fire" by Tim Hughes
- "Breathe" by Marie Barnett

Closing Challenge

Pastor: God has invited you to meet with him. He has provided for your redemption, he has restored you and brought you into a close relationship with him, and he has called you to tell everyone you know about his glorious invitation. Take him with you as you go throughout the wilderness of your life. Be the tabernacle of God to everyone you meet.

Worship Blueprint 9

Excavating the Soul

Theme
Letting God excavate the dirt from our souls

Goal
To help people remove obstacles between themselves and God so they can experience new life and healing

Scripture
Proverbs 20:9

SUMMARY OF THE EXPERIENCE

Mood: introspective

Synopsis: An offstage narrator tells the story of how sin and distractions seem to have separated him (or her) from God, as if he has buried his heart and soul deep below ground. Another person (representing God) enters and begins to dig in a container of dirt as the narrative continues to unfold. Finally, he bends over and pulls a shiny object from the dirt. The object represents the narrator's heart. "God" cleans it off and holds it close. Congregation members are then invited to come to the dirt to find their own "hearts" that God has excavated.

*Who can say, "I have kept
my heart pure; I am clean
and without sin"?*

—Proverbs 20:9

What people will

    see: a person digging, shiny objects

    hear: sounds of digging

    smell: dirt

    touch: dirt, shiny objects

    do: dig through dirt, sing

CREATING AN ENVIRONMENT FOR WORSHIP

Simple Environment

Place a trowel and a wheelbarrow full of dirt on a sheet of plastic. Place enough symbols of the human heart in the dirt for each person to find one. (You'll need one wheelbarrow and trowel for every 25 worshippers.)

Supplies for a Simple Environment

- person to enact the "Excavating the Soul" drama (pp. 71-75) (This script is also available as a printable download on the CD-ROM, segment 9A.)
- person to narrate the drama offstage
- leader to interact with the drama (Be sure to schedule time for this person to rehearse so that his or her digging coincides with the sound effects.)
- wheelbarrow of dirt or potting soil
- shovel or trowel
- shiny object representing the human heart—a coin, a marble, or a polished stone, for example (You'll need one for each attendee, plus about 25 percent more.)

- CD-ROM:
  Audio Track 4, the "Digging" sound effects
  "Blueprint 9" folder:
  - 9A, "Excavating the Soul" script

Maximum Environment

For this experience, the entire meeting area should be quite dark, with a spotlight on the person representing God. At the front of the meeting area, place a large sheet of heavy plastic to protect your floor. On top of it, place a large, flat box that can hold dirt. The box should be large enough to allow a person to stand in it and dig with a shovel—at least 3 feet wide, 3 feet long, and 1 foot deep.

To create an even more powerful environment, place excavation equipment—such as jackhammers, shovels, construction barricades, and caution tape—around the meeting area.

Additional Supplies for Maximizing the Experience
- large sheet of heavy plastic
- large, flat box
- shovels
- jackhammers
- construction barricades
- caution tape

9A "Excavating the Soul" Drama, Part 1

The worship area is nearly dark.

Narrator: *(Offstage)* Where have I hidden my heart from you, O Lord? *(Pause.)* I have buried it deep within my being, far from you. I have separated my heart from your presence, or so I thought.

Lord, I laid my heart on the ground. That's how it first got so dirty. My own desires drew my heart away from you and into the dirt. Then more and more dirt fell on my heart as my desires led to sin and drew me farther away from you. At first it didn't seem so bad, but now I realize that all the dirt on my heart has blocked me from your light.

The loneliest moment was when I could no longer see your light at all. My sin had become a deadness I brought on myself.

My soul was a dark place, far from you—buried under layers and layers of self-serving. My soul became the coffin of my heart.

I don't like it here. I try and try to dig myself out of this grave that I've buried myself in. I claw at the dirt, to no avail. What will save me now? How can I again reach the light of your presence and love? Lord, please come and set my heart free. Lift it from this dark place. Lord, please dig through the levels of separation that I have put between us. Please excavate my soul!

A spotlight illuminates the container of dirt. A person walks to the dirt with a shovel or trowel and begins to dig, slowly turning over each shovelful.

Begin playing Audio Track 4, the "Digging" sound effects. Continue playing these sound effects throughout the drama, pausing only during the song sets.

Narrator: Jesus said where your treasure is, there your heart will be also. What we make our treasure becomes our master. Lord, you know I didn't mean to treasure so many things more than you. *(Pause.)* But I did. It's my fault. What can be done for a rebellious heart like mine?

Leader: *(Offstage or onstage)* We allow so many things, so many desires to come between our hearts and God. But the good news is that nothing can keep you from God when you call on him to "excavate your soul." Today you have a chance to allow God to dig through all the sin and dirt in your life to uncover your heart and hold it close to his. Travel with us on a journey to the center of your soul.

"Excavating the Soul" Drama, Part 2

Narrator: *(Encouraged)* The first layer that must be dug through is pride. I stop myself from truly connecting with God in worship because I worry about how others will look at me. I want to connect with you, but I'm not comfortable singing, clapping, or raising my hands in a room full of people. It's more than that, though. Something in me doesn't want to admit I'm so far from you. And something in me doesn't want to relinquish control by letting myself be held in your hands. That's my pride. But, Lord, I want to change. Right now, Lord, I lay my pride before you. I don't want my heart to be separated from you by pride. I offer that shovelful of dirt to you right now and trust that your love can reach my heart.

Leader: Take a moment to silently invite God through that layer of pride.

Allow a moment of silence, except for the continued sound of digging.

Song Set 1

Stop Audio Track 4 as you move into Song Set 1. Select songs about God removing pride, such as these:

- "Surrender" by Marc James
- "Jesus, Draw Me Close" by Rick Founds
- "All My Life" by Libby Huirua, Wayne Huirua, and Mark DeJong
- "Your Love Is Deep" by Jami Smith, Dan Collins, and Susanna Bussey

"Excavating the Soul" Drama, Part 3

Resume Audio Track 4, the "Digging" sound effects.

Narrator: The next layer covering my soul is something I don't like to hear about: sin. Just like the packed earth, sin piles up, layer upon layer, burying all that comes under it. Sometimes I fear that my desires have gotten the best of me and that I will never truly experience intimacy with God. I know that on my own I cannot break the power of sin in my life.

But God said he never rests in the pursuit of our hearts. No sin or number of sins is too much for God. He longs to till and cultivate my soul. God will remove the sin that separates me from him if I let him. God wants me to invite him to dig through the layers of sin that separate my heart from his. Your love, O Lord, can reach my heart!

Leader: Let's silently ask God to break through the second layer of our separation: sin.

Allow several quiet moments in which people hear only the sound of digging.

Song Set 2

Stop Audio Track 4 as you move into Song Set 2. Select songs about God removing sin, such as these:
- "The Power of Your Love" by Geoff Bullock
- "Refiner's Fire" by Brian Doerksen
- "You Are My All in All" by Dennis Jernigan
- "Here I Am to Worship" by Tim Hughes

"Excavating the Soul" Drama, Part 4

Resume Audio Track 4, the "Digging" sound effects.

Narrator: As God continues to dig deep into my soul, his shovel hits the bedrock where my loyalties rest. The bedrock consists of whatever I treasure more than him.

It's one thing to admire God from a distance, but it's another to kneel at his feet and pledge myself to him. In the past I've given him a little of my time and a tiny bit of my treasure but nothing very significant. But I know that where my time and my money are, there is my treasure—there is my heart. So he asks me to honor him with both. I've resisted, but I've found that when I give God the things most precious to me, he unearths that layer of bedrock from my soul and uses it to lay the foundation for my faith. God wants digging rights on the deepest level of my loyalties. He wants to be my treasure. Your love, O Lord, can reach my heart.

Leader: In silence, let's ask God to break through that third layer of separation: our loyalties.

Allow several quiet moments in which people hear only the sound of digging.

Stop Audio Track 4 as you move into Song Set 3.

Song Set 3

Select songs about loyalty to God, such as these:
- "The Heart of Worship" by Matt Redman
- "Jesus, Lover of my Soul" by Paul Oakley

"Excavating the Soul" Drama, Part 5

Narrator: After digging deep into my soul—through my pride, through my sin, through my loyalties—God uncovers my heart.

The man who is digging stops, reaches down, and pulls something shiny from the dirt. Lights come on to brighten the whole scene around him. His actions then follow the narrator's words.

Narrator: When my heart is in God's hands, I celebrate, and so does he! The treasure that was hidden in the dirt has become truly God's. It's the most valuable treasure the world has ever

known; the only treasure that lasts. God's excavation makes way for my heart to bask in his amazing light, bringing new life and healing. He takes the heart I've placed in his hands, carefully cleans it off, and then holds it close to his own. My heart begins to beat strong again. My heart has found its true home, close to the heart of God.

Leader: If you will let him, God will hold your heart close to his. God has removed the barriers. Are you ready for God to hold your heart close to his own? If so, come up and dig your own heart from the dirt that God has excavated. As you do, thank God for removing the dirt from your heart so he can hold it close to his.

The person playing God exits. Encourage people to come forward and sift through the dirt with their hands to find their "hearts." Allow a few moments for people to reflect and pray before they return to their seats.

Leader: Pour out your heart to God now.

Song Set 4

Select songs about giving our hearts to God, such as these:
- "Lord, You Have My Heart" by Martin Smith
- "Be the Centre" by Michael Frye
- "With My Whole Heart" by Jeff E. Coleman

Conclusion

Close with a challenge and prayer.

Worship Blueprint 10

Face to Face With God's Holiness

Theme

Examining our lives in the light of God's holiness

Goal

To help worshippers come face to face with the holiness of God, respond to his power over their sin, and take the message of his cleansing power to their friends

Scriptures

Deuteronomy 4:24a; Deuteronomy 4:31; Deuteronomy 7:9; Deuteronomy 10:17; 1 Samuel 2:2; 2 Samuel 22:3b; Job 36:22; Psalm 18:2; Psalm 46:1-3; Psalm 47:7; Psalm 62:8; Psalm 84:11; Isaiah 6:1-8; Zephaniah 3:17; Revelation 4:8

SUMMARY OF THE EXPERIENCE

Mood: introspective

Synopsis: In this experience, people will hear readings about God's holiness and reflect on his Word. They'll hold rough sandpaper and relate it to the sin in their lives. They'll view a video intended to stimulate their thinking about their own sin. They'll also touch the fabric-covered back of the sandpaper and relate its

"Woe to me!" I cried. "I am ruined! For I am a man of unclean lips, and I live among a people of unclean lips, and my eyes have seen the King, the Lord Almighty."
—Isaiah 6:5

smoothness to the forgiveness available through Jesus. Finally, they'll write short letters describing God's love.

What people will

    see: "Ashamed?" video

    hear: "Holy, Holy, Holy" dramatic reading

    touch: rough squares of sandpaper backed with smooth fabric

    do: interact with Scriptures through a guided meditation, consider their sin and God's holiness, and write letters to their friends about God

CREATING AN ENVIRONMENT FOR WORSHIP

Simple Environment

Increase the space between seats to allow as much privacy as possible for each participant. Lower the lights, and light as many candles as possible.

Supplies for a Simple Environment
- 4 readers for the "Holy, Holy, Holy" dramatic reading (pp. 80-81) (This dramatic reading is also available as a printable download on the CD-ROM, segment 10A.)
- reader for the "Isaiah 6:1-6" guided meditation (p. 82)

(This is also available as a printable download on the CD-ROM, segment 10B.)

- leader to interact with the congregation during the worship experience
- enough "texture squares" for each worshipper to have one (Use spray glue to glue red felt or satin onto the back of sheets of rough sandpaper. Cut 2-inch squares of the felt- or satin-backed sandpaper.)
- volunteers to distribute items during the experience
- sheet of stationery for each worshipper
- pens
- candles
- CD-ROM:
  "Blueprint 10" folder:
  - 10A, "Holy, Holy, Holy" dramatic reading
  - 10B, "Isaiah 6:1-6" guided meditation
  - 10C, "Ashamed?" video
  - 10D, "Holy, Holy, Holy" lyrics (optional)
  - 10E, "Take My Life and Let It Be" lyrics (optional)

Maximum Environment

Increase the space between seats to allow as much privacy as possible for each participant. Lower the lights, and light as many candles as possible.

Isaiah 6:1-8 describes seraphim proclaiming God's holiness. Surround your church with a proclamation of God's holiness by creating a praise banner that will stretch around the entire worship area. Purchase enough muslin to make one trip around the worship area. Using fabric pens, cover the muslin with words describing God, focusing on his holiness. You may repeat some of the words and phrases again and again—"God is holy," "God is awesome," "Holy, holy, holy is the Lord God almighty," for example. Invite your church's Sunday school or Bible study groups to help create the banner.

Additional Supplies for Maximizing the Experience
- muslin
- fabric pens
- volunteers to create a banner

THE EXPERIENCE

Song Set 1

Select upbeat to medium-tempo songs about God's holiness, such as these:

10D • "Holy, Holy, Holy" by Reginald Heber
  • "Open the Eyes of My Heart" by Paul Baloche
  • "Holy Is the Lord" by Chris Tomlin and Louie Giglio

10A "Holy, Holy, Holy" Dramatic Reading

In this readers' theater, each reader should be familiar with the script, but none of it has to be memorized. Tell readers not to read the italicized Scripture references. Revelation 4:8 is repeated several times; ask the readers to practice varying the way they present this verse. As different parts of the verse are stressed, different meanings emerge.

Reader 1: "Holy, holy, holy is the Lord God Almighty, who was, and is, and is to come" *(Revelation 4:8).*

Reader 2: "The Lord your God is a consuming fire" *(Deuteronomy 4:24a).*

Reader 3: "The Lord your God is a merciful God; he will not abandon or destroy you or forget the covenant with your forefathers, which he confirmed to them by oath" *(Deuteronomy 4:31).*

Reader 4: "Know therefore that the Lord your God is God; he is the faithful God, keeping his covenant of love to a thousand generations of those who love him and keep his commands" *(Deuteronomy 7:9).*

Reader 2: "Holy, holy, holy is the Lord God Almighty, who was, and is, and is to come" *(Revelation 4:8).*

Reader 1: "For the Lord your God is God of gods and Lord of lords, the great God, mighty and awesome, who shows no partiality and accepts no bribes" *(Deuteronomy 10:17).*

Reader 3: "There is no one holy like the Lord; there is no one besides you; there is no Rock like our God" *(1 Samuel 2:2).* "He is my stronghold, my refuge and my savior" *(2 Samuel 22:3b).*

Reader 4: "God is exalted in his power. Who is a teacher like him?" *(Job 36:22).*

Reader 3: "Holy, holy, holy is the Lord God Almighty, who was, and is, and is to come" *(Revelation 4:8)*.

Reader 2: "The Lord is my rock, my fortress and my deliverer; my God is my rock, in whom I take refuge. He is my shield and the horn of my salvation, my stronghold" *(Psalm 18:2)*.

Reader 4: "God is our refuge and strength, an ever-present help in trouble. Therefore we will not fear, though the earth give way and the mountains fall into the heart of the sea, though its waters roar and foam and the mountains quake with their surging" *(Psalm 46:1-3)*.

Reader 1: "For God is the King of all the earth; sing to him a psalm of praise" *(Psalm 47:7)*.

Reader 4: "Holy, holy, holy is the Lord God Almighty, who was, and is, and is to come" *(Revelation 4:8)*.

Reader 2: "Trust in him at all times, O people; pour out your hearts to him, for God is our refuge" *(Psalm 62:8)*.

Reader 1: "For the Lord God is a sun and shield; the Lord bestows favor and honor; no good thing does he withhold from those whose walk is blameless" *(Psalm 84:11)*.

Reader 3: "The Lord your God is with you, he is mighty to save. He will take great delight in you, he will quiet you with his love, he will rejoice over you with singing" *(Zephaniah 3:17)*.

All: "Holy, holy, holy is the Lord God Almighty, who was, and is, and is to come" *(Revelation 4:8)*.

Pastor: We often speak about the *holiness* of God. In fact, we toss the word *holiness* around so much that it's easy to forget what it means. But when we truly come face to face with the holiness of God, three things happen: We begin to realize how great God is, we realize how sinful we are, and we want to tell everyone about God's greatness. It is our hope that through worship today you will come face to face with God's holiness, and through that encounter you will leave here ready to share his love and holiness with everyone you meet.

10B "Isaiah 6:1-6" Guided Meditation

In our services, we tend to quickly read the text on our way to the message. In this guided meditation, participants will meditate on the text for an extended period of time, focusing on God's holiness.

Begin by reading the following paragraph. Then read Isaiah 6:1-6, and allow a time of silence. The length of this silence will vary, but it's a good idea to extend the silence longer than is comfortable. After the silence, read the next paragraph. Then read Isaiah 6:1-6 again, and allow another time of silence. Repeat the process once more after reading the last paragraph. (Wait at least two and a half minutes between each reading, longer if you can. Two minutes will seem like an eternity, so use a watch to time the silences.)

Pastor: Close your eyes, bow your head, and breathe in slowly through your nose. Hold your breath for a moment. *(Pause.)* Now let it out. Ask God to reveal his holy words to you. *(Pause.)* As I read this passage, don't think about it; just listen. Feel the rhythm and the power of God's words. Don't analyze them; just experience them.

Read Isaiah 6:1-6; then allow a lengthy silence.

This time, as I read the Scripture, imagine that you're in Isaiah's place. Think about how you would respond to the sights and sounds that he describes. Let the words God spoke to Isaiah truly speak to you.

Read Isaiah 6:1-6; then allow a lengthy silence.

Now, as I read the Scripture again, listen for certain words or phrases that jump out at you. Repeat these words or phrases silently. Ask God to speak directly to your heart through these words.

Read Isaiah 6:1-6; then allow a lengthy silence.

Song Set 2

Select slower songs, such as any of the following, focusing on God's holiness and humanity's sinfulness.

- "Agnus Dei" by Michael W. Smith
- "We Fall Down" by Chris Tomlin
- "Break Our Hearts" by Billy Foote
- "Facedown" by Matt Redman

The Feel of Sin

Cue volunteers to distribute a texture square to each worshipper.

Pastor: Place the square on your knee, sandpaper side up, and run your fingers over the surface. Feel the roughness. When we come face to face with our holy God, we will always become more aware of the sin in our lives. Right now think of your sins as the bumps in the sandpaper. As you pass your fingers over the surface, ask God to make you aware of your sins and of your need for his holiness. Ask God to help you see him as he truly is and yourself as you truly are.

Give worshippers a few moments to do this as soft background music plays. Then read Genesis 3:6-8.

"Ashamed?" Video

10C Immediately after the Scripture reading, play the "Ashamed?" video. At the conclusion of the video, read Genesis 3:21 and Isaiah 6:5-6.

The Feel of Forgiveness

Pastor: In the light of God's holiness, our sin is unbearably dark and shameful. But here's the amazing thing: Even though we've messed up, God has provided a way for us to make our way back to him. For Adam and Eve, God killed an animal and made clothing. For us, God sent his Son, Jesus, to die for us and cover our shame—to make us clean. Romans 5:8 tells us that while we were still sinners, while we were still powerless to do anything, before we were good enough or smart enough or pretty enough or powerful enough, Christ died for us. It is through that sacrificial death that we are able to draw near to God.

Now turn the sandpaper over,
and touch the side covered in fabric. Feel its smoothness.
Think about Jesus' death. His death means that your sins can be
forgiven and the roughness of your life can be made smooth.

If you've never asked Jesus to forgive your sins, take time to
do it now. If you'd like, talk to one of our counselors. If you have
already asked Jesus for his forgiveness, then spend this time
thanking God for this amazing gift.

*As soft music plays, provide time for people to pray and seek
counsel as they consider God's forgiveness.*

Song Set 3 (optional)

You may wish to extend the time for people to consider God's
forgiveness by singing or playing a few soft songs such as the
following:
- "Once Again" by Matt Redman
- "You Are My King" by Billy Foote

How, Then, Shall We Respond?

Pastor: When Isaiah saw the Lord, he came face to face with his own sin and God's awesome holiness. Once God made him clean, Isaiah was given a task.

Read Isaiah 6:6-8.

When we come face to face with God's holiness, we first recognize our need for God's cleansing touch. Then we are invited to share the message of that touch with others. God is standing in this place, offering you forgiveness and inviting you to join him on this great adventure. This very day, he's asking, "Whom shall I send? And who will go for us?" How will you respond?

As we close, I want to give you a chance to begin saying to God, "Here am I. Send me!"

Writing Letters

Pastor: Who do you know who needs to hear about God's amazing holiness and love? Spend a few minutes asking God with whom you should share this amazing news; then write that person a short letter encouraging him or her and sharing God's amazing love.

Cue volunteers to distribute stationery and pens. Play soft, contemplative music as people write letters explaining how God has affected their lives. Allow at least six minutes for them to compose their letters.

After sufficient time has elapsed, ask people to form pairs or trios and pray for those who will receive their letters. If your tradition allows, you might have people lay their hands on their letters and on each other as a way of commissioning them to share God's love with their friends.

Closing Songs

Close by singing one or two soft praise songs. It would be good to begin with the song that was playing softly as people were praying. You might also consider the following choices:

- "Take My Life" by Scott Underwood
- "Take My Life, Lead Me, Lord" by R. Maines Rawls
- **10E** • "Take My Life and Let It Be" by Frances R. Havergal

Closing Charge

Read Isaiah 6:1-8.

Pastor: You have seen the holiness of God and have been made aware of your own sin. You have also seen that God himself forgives you and cleanses you of your sins. Take those images and thoughts with you this week. Leave here knowing the forgiving holiness of God, and tell everyone you meet how they, too, can know God.

Worship Blueprint 11

Fear of Commitment

Theme

Fulfilling and embracing the commitments we've made to others and to God

Goal

To help people understand the importance of the commitments they've made and to help them renew those commitments

Scriptures

Psalm 37:5-6; Matthew 5:37

SUMMARY OF THE EXPERIENCE

Mood: weddinglike

Synopsis: As congregants enter the worship area, they'll find it set up for a wedding ceremony and will be treated as wedding guests. After the "bride" and "groom" have taken their places in front of the congregation, the pastor will begin to administer the vows. But the wedding will begin to melt down as the bride begins to have second thoughts and finally leaves the room in a panic. This will introduce the message on the fear of commitment.

*Simply let your "Yes" be "Yes,"
and your "No," "No"; anything
beyond this comes from the
evil one.*
　　　　　　—Matthew 5:37

What people will

see: a wedding party, candles, a "bride's" meltdown

hear: wedding songs, vows

do: participate in a mock wedding ceremony, pray for one
another's relationships

CREATING AN ENVIRONMENT FOR WORSHIP

Simple Environment

Ask the "bride" to wear a white dress or suit and the "groom" to
wear a suit and tie.

Supplies for a Simple Environment

- person to play the part of a bride (See the "Meltdown" script,
pp. 90-91.)
- person to play the part of a groom
- CD-ROM:
"Blueprint 11" folder:
  - 11A, "Joyful, Joyful, We Adore Thee" lyrics (optional)
  - 11B, "All Hail the Power of Jesus' Name" lyrics (optional)
  - 11C, "Meltdown" script
  - 11D, "Great Is Thy Faithfulness" lyrics (optional)

Maximum Environment

Go all out! Design the bulletin to resemble a wedding program.
Set up seating in two major sections divided by a center aisle. (If
your church has fixed seating, set up your worship space as you

normally do for a wedding.) Arrange for wedding candelabra and candle lighters. Provide a bouquet for the bride, and decorate the worship area with flowers. Set up a guest book and other wedding items outside the worship area so people will see them as they enter. After the guests have been seated, roll out a full-length aisle runner.

Encourage the "bride" and "groom" to dress in elaborate wedding attire. Recruit men and women to play the roles of groomsmen and bridesmaids, and encourage them to dress as elaborately as possible. Ask every usher to wear a suit or dress, and give each a boutonniere or corsage. Ask the pastor to dress in the most formal attire acceptable in your church.

Additional Supplies for Maximizing the Experience

- bulletins designed like wedding programs
- wedding candelabra
- volunteers to act as candle lighters
- guest book
- volunteer to attend to the guest book
- aisle runner
- volunteers to dress in elaborate wedding attire

THE EXPERIENCE

Prelude

As congregants enter the worship area, play traditional wedding songs such as "Jesu, Joy of Man's Desiring," Pachelbel's "Canon," "Ode to Joy," and "The Wedding Song."

As ushers greet attendees and give them programs, they ask each person, "Would you prefer to sit on the side of the bride or the groom?" People might answer or look perplexed. If the latter, ushers suggest a side and then show people to their seats. When it's time to begin the service, two ushers come forward and light the candles.

Song Set 1

The pastor or worship leader enters, welcomes everyone to the wedding, and asks people to stand and sing one or two majestic songs (such as those listed below), accompanied by a full-pipes sound from a keyboard or an organ.

11A • "Joyful, Joyful, We Adore Thee" by Henry Van Dyke

11B • "All Hail the Power of Jesus' Name" by Edward Perronet

At the completion of the songs, the pastor or worship leader asks the congregation to be seated.

The Processional

As the keyboardist plays a traditional processional song, the pastor, groom, and any other members of the wedding party enter, stand in front, and wait for the bride's entrance.

The pastor asks everyone to rise as the keyboardist plays "Here Comes the Bride." The bride walks slowly down the aisle.

The pastor performs an abbreviated wedding ceremony. At the appropriate time, the groom confidently says, "I do!" The bride looks around nervously as the pastor leads up to her vows. When it's time, she hesitates, then says a quick "I do." Then her meltdown begins.

11C "Meltdown" Script

The bride turns to face the congregation; the rest of the wedding party freezes in place, oblivious to her words.

Bride: Thanks for coming to my wedding, but you can leave now if you want. I'm not really getting married today. *(Turns back toward pastor for a few seconds, then faces audience again.)*

Don't tell him *(nods toward groom)*. He's a great guy and all, but I'm just not ready to get married. *(Turns toward pastor for a few seconds, then faces audience again.)*

This is a scary thing, you know. Marriage. Lifelong faithfulness. In just a few hours, he'd realize he's married to a nutcase, and he'd be ready to kill me! *(Turns toward pastor for a few seconds, then turns back to audience.)*

This is just too much commitment for me. He's going to expect a lot from me, like picking up his dirty socks, and…well, you know *(rolling her eyes)*. I'm afraid of how it will all end up.

I might not make it, so I might as well not start. *(Turns toward pastor for a few seconds, then turns back to audience.)*

Thanks for the gifts—keep them or give them to someone else. You can all go home now. Don't forget to take a piece of cake with you. Be happy. Forget this ever happened. *(Turns toward pastor.)*

Groom: *(Loudly)* With this ring…

Bride: *(Turns to audience)* I am *not* getting married!

Groom: I thee wed. *(Starts to slip ring on bride's finger.)*

Bride looks at groom for a moment, pulls her hand back, screams, and runs down the aisle and out of the worship space.

Lights go out. Wedding party exits.

Lights come back up; pastor removes garments not normally worn during a worship service and begins the message.

Message

Consider using any of the following points in the message:

- Compare the bride's lack of commitment to the groom to people's lack of commitment to God.
- Ask people to seriously consider the nature of their commitments to God. Are they faithfully committed, or are they "casually dating"? Do they get together with God once a week and enjoy his company without taking the relationship seriously?
- Although we may fear commitment, God wants us to be totally committed—to him and to our spouses.
- When we make commitments to other people, such as our spouses and our children, we are also making those commitments to God.
- Breaking commitments affects our relationships with God as well as our human relationships. God wants us to be faithful to *all* our commitments.

- When we make commitments to God, he promises us that "he will make [our] righteousness shine like the dawn, the justice of [our] cause like the noonday sun" (Psalm 37:6).

Song Set 2

Choose from as many of the following as you wish:
- "I Could Sing of Your Love Forever" by Martin Smith
- "Faithful" by Ben Pasley and Robin Pasley
- "I Will Offer Up My Life" by Matt Redman
- "Surrender" by Marc James
- "Beautiful One" by Tim Hughes
- "Enough" by Chris Tomlin and Louie Giglio

11D • "Great Is Thy Faithfulness" by Thomas O. Chisholm

Closing

The service ends with a time of community worship. As the band or a recording plays Passion's song "We Are Hungry," half of the congregation stands and sings the first verse and chorus while the other half prays for the marriages and relationships of those standing and singing. Upon completion of the first chorus, the two halves switch roles and continue. After each half has sung and prayed, the pastor or worship leader invites everyone to finish the song together.

The service ends with a closing challenge and prayer.

Worship Blueprint **12**

Hope

Theme
Realizing the hope that the first Easter gives us

Goal
To clearly explain why Christ followers view Easter as special and to invite people to indicate where they are in their spiritual journeys

Scripture
Luke 24

SUMMARY OF THE EXPERIENCE

Mood: celebratory at the beginning, moving into reflective and contemplative

Synopsis: This Easter experience is intended not only to remind people that Jesus rose from the dead but also to invite them into a relationship with him. People are invited to sign rocks signifying where they are on their spiritual journeys.

This is what is written: The Christ will suffer and rise from the dead on the third day, and repentance and forgiveness of sins will be preached in his name to all nations.

—*Luke 24:46b-47a*

What people will

see: an altar and small rocks

hear: soft music

smell: incense

touch: rocks

do: sign rocks to signify where they are in their spiritual journeys

CREATING AN ENVIRONMENT FOR WORSHIP

Simple Environment

Drape burlap or another type of rough fabric over an existing altar or a table. Place a few candles and incense on the table and on the floor around the table. Stack small rocks around the altar so people can each take one, sign it, and set it on the altar. Place a basket of black markers on the altar. If you have a larger number of people, you may want to set up multiple stations to avoid crowding.

Supplies for a Simple Environment

- altar
- rough fabric such as burlap
- candles
- incense

- small rocks, each about the size of an egg (You'll need enough for each person to take one.)
- basket
- black markers
- a person to describe an especially meaningful Easter experience

Maximum Environment

The visual symbolism of a hand-built altar can be powerful. Maintain an earthy feel for the altar and all the elements that go with it. For example, you could use wood, cinderblocks, bricks, or large rocks to build the altar. Pour sand into clay pots, and place incense in the sand. Place black markers in smaller clay pots, and place them around the altar along with the incense. Place small rocks in two or three large clay pots. If you have other props in the room for your Easter celebration, make sure these items work well with the appearance and feel of the altar.

Additional Supplies for Maximizing the Experience
- hand-built altar using earthy materials
- sand
- clay pots

The Experience

Opening Music

Play soft, low-key music.

Song Set 1

- "Meet With Me" by Lamont Hiebert
- "Not to Us" by Jesse Reeves and Chris Tomlin

Featured Song

"In Christ Alone" by Stuart Townend and Keith Getty

Message, Part 1

Consider using any of the following points in the message:

- Jesus' death and resurrection truly happened.
- Without Jesus' death, there would be no forgiveness of sin.
- Without Jesus' resurrection, there would be no hope of our resurrection.
- The events of that first Easter give us hope that we can't find anywhere else.

Featured Song

"Blessed Be Your Name" by Matt Redman and Beth Redman

Personal Story

Arrange for someone to share a personal story about his or her spiritual journey. Ideally, this person became a Christ follower or reached another turning point in his or her spiritual journey at a previous Easter service. Ask the person to describe how that experience affected his or her life. (Personal stories can be very powerful if done well. To avoid the person rambling or going too long, be sure to ask the person to write his or her comments before the service and to read them from the platform.)

Message, Part 2

Explain that rock altars were used in the Old Testament to remind the people of Israel of significant events in their journeys with God. List several examples from the Old Testament. Explain that we are all on a spiritual journey and that we all connect with God in especially powerful ways at certain points along the way. Tell listeners that the altar on the platform has been provided to give people an opportunity to mark a point in their spiritual journeys. Tell them that they will be invited to approach the altar, pick up a rock, sign it, and leave it at the altar. Explain that signing a rock could signify the beginning of a relationship with God or it could signify a recommitment to this relationship or a next step in the relationship.

Song Set 2

Invite people to sign a rock as the band or a recording plays "Worth It All" by Rita Springer. Allow plenty of time for people to sign rocks, reflect, and pray, playing additional music if necessary.

Closing

Conclude with prayer. As people leave, have the band or a recording play "In Christ Alone" by Stuart Townend and Keith Getty.

Worship Blueprint 13

Intentional Living

Theme

Being intentional with our skills and time

Goal

To encourage people to examine how nearly they are living up to their potential

Scriptures

Judges 6; Proverbs 16:2-3; Proverbs 19:21; Isaiah 32:8; Jeremiah 29:11; Romans 8:28; 1 Corinthians 9:24-27; Philippians 2:1-5; Philippians 3:13-14

SUMMARY OF THE EXPERIENCE

Mood: quiet and reflective

Synopsis: Worshippers enter a softly lit worship area designed for quiet contemplation and are then challenged to think about their purpose in life. Scriptures encouraging them to fulfill their potential as Christ followers are woven throughout the service, along with opportunities to respond in writing to questions related to those Scriptures. The experience also includes worship songs, a movie clip, offstage reading, and reflective music.

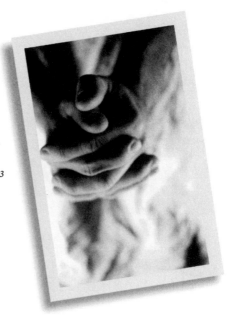

*Commit to the Lord
whatever you do, and your
plans will succeed.*
—Proverbs 16:3

What people will

> **see:** a softly lit worship area, Scriptures and thought-provoking questions on the screen, a movie clip

> **hear:** reflective music, an offstage voice leading them through the experience

> **do:** write their responses to challenging questions about their purpose in life

CREATING AN ENVIRONMENT FOR WORSHIP

Simple Environment

Because the CD-ROM is used extensively throughout this service, much of your preparation time should be spent making sure all the elements of the service flow together and will engage everyone. Be sure the offstage reader has a pleasant voice and speaks well in public.

Lower the lights in the worship area, and distribute sheets of paper and pens to people as they arrive. Play soft background music during journaling times.

Supplies for a Simple Environment
- person to read offstage
- sheet of paper and pen for each worshipper
- soft lighting

• CD-ROM:

  "Blueprint 13" folder:
  - 13A, PowerPoint presentation (Please be sure to use
    PowerPoint Viewer 2003, which can be downloaded from
    Microsoft at no cost. For detailed information, see the
    "Read Me" file on the CD-ROM.)
• *Parenthood* movie clip and the appropriate license for
  showing it (Cue the movie to 1:49:42, when Gil says, "Isn't
  that demented?" End it at 1:55:59 as Gil hugs his wife.) In this
  scene, Grandma describes two different rides at an amusement
  park and compares them to people's lives. Gil doesn't
  understand what she's getting at but finally understands that
  it's better to take risks in life than to always play it safe.

Maximum Environment

Because the CD-ROM is used extensively throughout this
service, much of your preparation time should be devoted to
making sure all the elements of the service flow together and will
engage everyone. Be sure the offstage reader has a pleasant voice
and speaks well in public.

Create a journal for each participant by assembling two or
three sheets of paper between two pieces of cardboard backing
and clipping them together with attractive clips. Place pens in
attractive holders that coordinate with the other props. Set up
small tables throughout the worship area, and place journals and
pens on each table. (Be sure to position the tables so people have
easy access to the pens and journals.) You can use different sizes
and shapes of tables, but cover them with fabric so they all have
the same look.

Lighting is key in setting the mood for this experience. Turn
off the overhead lights, and set table lamps and floor lamps
with low-wattage bulbs around the worship area to create the
ambience of a reading room. Try to use lamps that complement
the other props.

Music is another key component. Plan soft background music
for the journaling times.

Additional Supplies for Maximizing the Experience

• handmade journal for each participant

- holders for pens
- small tables
- fabric to cover tables
- table and floor lamps

The Experience

Song Set 1
- "No One Like You" by David Crowder, Jack Parker, Jason Solley, Jeremy Bush, Mike Dodson, and Mike Hogan
- "Hallelujah" by Brenton Brown and Brian Doerksen

Scripture Journey, Part 1

Offstage Voice: Do you have a clear purpose for your life—one that consumes your every thought, engages your passions, and is big enough to keep you focused for the rest of your life? Think about what that purpose might be.

13A PowerPoint Presentation

Play soft background music as people contemplate the Scriptures on the screen.

Slide 1

Philippians 2:1-2

"If you have any encouragement from being united with Christ, if any comfort from his love, if any fellowship with the Spirit, if any tenderness and compassion, then make my joy complete by being like-minded, having the same love, being one in spirit and purpose."

Slide 2

Philippians 2:3-5

"Do nothing out of selfish ambition or vain conceit, but in humility consider others better than yourselves. Each of you should look not only to your own interests, but also to the interests of others. Your attitude should be the same as that of Christ Jesus."

Slide 3

Romans 8:28

"And we know that in all things God works for the good of those who love him, who have been called according to his purpose."

Journaling

Tell people to contemplate the questions on the screen and to write down their thoughts. Play soft background music as people journal.

Slide 4

- What's the most important thing you can do with your life?
- What things in your life now are worth your effort? What things are not?

Scripture Journey, Part 2

Offstage Voice: It's often been said that if you aim at nothing, you're sure to hit it. When he was 15, John Goddard created a list of 127 goals that he wanted to achieve within his lifetime. Some of those goals were to fly an airplane, write a book, and explore the Nile River. By the time he was 74, John had achieved 109 of his goals. Think about the goals you're striving toward as you contemplate the following Scriptures.

Contemplation

Play soft background music as people contemplate the Scriptures on the screen.

Slide 5

1 Corinthians 9:24-25

"Do you not know that in a race all the runners run, but only one gets the prize? Run in such a way as to get the prize. Everyone who competes in the games goes into strict training. They do it to get a crown that will not last; but we do it to get a crown that will last forever."

Slide 6

1 Corinthians 9:26-27

"Therefore I do not run like a man running aimlessly; I do not fight like a man beating the air. No, I beat my body and make it my slave so that after I have preached to others, I myself will not be disqualified for the prize."

Journaling

Tell people to contemplate the questions on the screen and to write down their thoughts. Play soft background music as people journal.

Slide 7

- What God-planted goals are growing within you?
- What secret ambitions are waiting for you to take action?

Parenthood Movie Clip

Ask the congregation to watch the movie clip and to consider the dilemma it poses. Play the clip.

Journaling

Tell people to contemplate the questions on the screen and to write down their thoughts. Play soft background music as people journal.

Slide 8
- What carnival ride best symbolizes your life: a merry-go-round or a roller coaster?
- Sometimes our fears prevent us from reaching our goals. What are three fears that are hindering your progress toward your goals?

Scripture Journey, Part 3

Offstage Voice: The story of Gideon demonstrates how God can take someone who lacks confidence in his ability and use him to do great things. God promised to be with Gideon, and he was. God looks for people who know they don't have it all together. They know that without God, they can't accomplish much. They're the ones who will rely on him.

Read Judges 6 aloud.

Contemplation

Play soft background music as people contemplate the Scriptures on the screen.

Slide 9
Proverbs 16:2-3
"All a man's ways seem innocent to him, but motives are weighed by the Lord. Commit to the Lord whatever you do, and your plans will succeed."

Slide 10
Proverbs 19:21
"Many are the plans in a man's heart, but it is the Lord's purpose that prevails."

Slide 11
Jeremiah 29:11
" 'For I know the plans I have for you,' declares the Lord, 'plans to prosper you and not to harm you, plans to give you hope and a future.' "

Featured Song

"World on Fire" by Sarah McLachlan and Pierre Marchand

Scripture Journey, Part 4

Offstage Voice: Honoring God is more important than anything else we do. It's the thing that should drive us and give meaning to our lives. People all around us are driven by other things and end up feeling empty at the end of the day—and at the end of life. We're meant to serve God. Only when we're doing that can we really accomplish anything.

Contemplation

Play soft background music as people contemplate the Scriptures on the screen.

Slide 12

Philippians 3:13-14

"Brothers, I do not consider myself yet to have taken hold of it. But one thing I do: Forgetting what is behind and straining toward what is ahead, I press on toward the goal to win the prize for which God has called me heavenward in Christ Jesus."

Song Set 2

- "We Are Hungry" by Brad Kilman
- "Holy Is the Lord" by Chris Tomlin and Louie Giglio

Prayer

Guide people in a time of prayer. Allow volunteers to pray aloud. End your service by telling worshippers to take their journals with them. Encourage them to reflect on what they've written and to continue writing during the coming week.

Worship Blueprint 14

Kerygma (Proclamation)

Theme

Discovering Christian worship through the ages

Goal

To celebrate God by worshipping in some of the various ways Christians have worshipped throughout the centuries

Scriptures

Psalm 63:1-4; Acts 20:7; Philippians 2:5-11

SUMMARY OF THE EXPERIENCE

Mood: reflective

Synopsis: Worshippers enter a darkened worship area that is designed to feel like a catacomb as a person onstage reads psalms of praise accompanied by ethereal background music.

Three easels and sets of art supplies are set up at the front of the worship area, each in clear view of the congregation. The leader invites three preselected artists to come forward and paint the idea of "worshipping through ancient-future eyes." Throughout the service, people watch as these three works of art take shape.

The leader then presents a brief message about the meaning and purpose of worship. At the end of the message, the worship

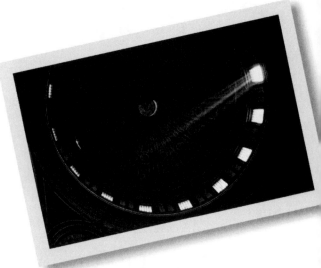

I have seen you in the sanctuary and beheld your power and your glory. Because your love is better than life, my lips will glorify you. I will praise you as long as I live, and in your name I will lift up my hands.

—Psalm 63:2-4

leader and a narrator lead the congregation through nine examples of worship representing Christianity throughout the centuries. Each time period is introduced by a PowerPoint image on the screen and a narrator's short description of that period and the type of worship that was prevalent then. Music in the style of that time is then played or sung. Here are the order of the time periods and the song and music options:

1. The Catacombs (A.D. 200), reflective acoustic music
2. The Celtic Period (750), "Be Thou My Vision" translated by Mary Byrne
3. The Latin Period (1265), "Kyrie Eleison"
4. The Reformation (1529), "A Mighty Fortress" by Martin Luther
5. The African-American Spiritual Period (1862), "Were You There"
6. The Gospel Period (1932), "I'll Fly Away" by Albert E. Brumley
7. The 1980s (1988), "Awesome God" by Rich Mullins
8. The 1990s (1991), "You're Worthy of My Praise" by David Ruis
9. The 2000s (2003), "Surrender" by Marc James

As the time of worship comes to an end, worshippers are invited to meet with the three artists after the service to discuss the paintings they've just created. The pastor closes with prayer.

What people will

    see: near darkness, ancient Christian symbols, images of various worship eras, paintings as they're being created

    hear: praise psalms, music from various periods of Christian worship

CREATING AN ENVIRONMENT FOR WORSHIP

Simple Environment

To help create an environment reminiscent of the catacombs, lower the lights as much as possible and use lots of candles. Place one large candle near the center of the stage, and light it during the "catacombs" portion of the worship experience. Paint large, ancient Christian symbols on paper, and hang them in the front of the worship area.

Supplies for a Simple Environment
- material for creating large, ancient Christian symbols
- person to read psalms of praise onstage before the service begins
- narrator
- music from different eras (Specific musical choices are up to you. We've suggested one piece to represent each era of worship, but if you want to use different selections, you certainly may do so.)
- painting supplies and easels for 3 artists (It's great to have a variety of mediums—watercolors, oils, and calligraphy, for example.)
- 3 artists
- candles
- CD-ROM:
  "Blueprint 14" folder:
  - 14A, PowerPoint presentation
  - 14B, "Philippians 2:5-11"
  - 14C, "Be Thou My Vision" lyrics
  - 14D, "A Mighty Fortress Is Our God" lyrics
  - 14E, "Were You There" lyrics
- digital photo of your community, captioned with the current year, that you can project on the screen

Maximum Environment

To help create an environment reminiscent of the catacombs, lower the lights as much as possible and use lots of candles. Place one large candle near the center of the stage, and light it during the "catacombs" portion of the worship experience. Create large, ancient Christian symbols, such as an ichthus and an empty tomb with the boulder rolled away, and place them near the front of the worship area so they are visible as people enter.

Additional Supplies for Maximizing the Experience
- ancient symbols of worship

THE EXPERIENCE

As people begin to enter the darkened worship area, they'll see a lone figure sitting on stage, thoughtfully reading aloud Psalms 145–150. The person will begin reading about 15 minutes before the service begins and will stop as the service begins. Back up the reader with quiet music, perhaps ethereal or Celtic instrumental selections from a CD.

Introduction

Introduce the topic—Christian worship through the ages—then point out the three large easels near the front of the worship area. Ask the three artists you've selected to move to the easels. Explain that they will be painting their ideas of what it means to "worship God through ancient-future eyes" throughout the service.

Message

Consider using any of the following points in the message:
- Introduce the message by exploring the meaning and purpose of worship. How does God view worship? What does God expect from us? What needs does worship fulfill in us?
- Explore the word *kerygma* (kay-roog-ma), the Latin word used in the New Testament to describe the proclamation of the gospel, the message that God shows grace and mercy to anyone who receives Jesus.

- Explain that what God did for us through Jesus is worth celebrating, and that's what we do when we worship and proclaim the good news of the grace of God.

Celebrating the Timeless God

The band, the worship leader, and the narrator take their places. The narrator introduces the experience to come.

Narrator: Come with us on a journey, a journey to connect with how Christians from the earliest days after Christ's resurrection celebrated God—what Jesus called "worshipping in Spirit and in truth."

Times and cultures have changed. National boundaries and entire nations have disappeared. People groups have changed. But the message that Jesus came to earth to live a sinless life, died on the cross as a sacrifice for our sins, rose again, and overcame death *has not changed* in 2,000 years.

God transcends space and time, and so does our worship of him. The book of Revelation tells us that people from all nations and languages will gather to worship God for all eternity. When we leave this earth, barriers of time, style, culture, and language will cease. All that will remain is the eternal community gathered forever to celebrate Jesus.

Take this journey with us, a journey in the ways and the words Christ followers have used for two millennia to approach and experience God, to sit at Jesus' feet and worship him.

14A PowerPoint Presentation

Slide 1: The Catacombs

Display the photo "Rome, Italy, A.D. 200" on the screen.

Narrator: The earliest record of Christian worship after Jesus left the earth was written during a time of great persecution. In the first century, the Roman government was trying to eradicate Christianity. This caused the early church to worship secretly in vaults or galleries in underground tombs; these were the catacombs. Christians met under the cover of darkness, identifying the place and time through ancient symbols such as the ones you see around us today. Amazingly enough, during this time of persecution and fear, the church grew faster than ever!

We don't know what their music sounded like, but we do know some of the words they sang. The lyrics of one of the hymns of the early church are recorded in Philippians 2:5-11. We're going to experience that hymn right now. The place: the catacombs near Rome, Italy. The year: A.D. 200.

Light a large candle in the center of the stage. Extinguish all other lights.

14B *Display the text of Philippians 2:5-11 on the screen as the narrator reads it aloud:*

"Your attitude should be the same as that of Christ Jesus: Who, being in very nature God, did not consider equality with God something to be grasped, but made himself nothing, taking the very nature of a servant, being made in human likeness. And being found in appearance as a man, he humbled himself and became obedient to death—even death on a cross! Therefore God exalted him to the highest place and gave him the name that is above every name, that at the name of Jesus every knee should bow, in heaven and on earth and under the earth, and every tongue confess that Jesus Christ is Lord, to the glory of God the Father."

Slide 2: The Celtic Period
Display the photo "Ireland 750" on the screen.

Narrator: In the early eighth century, Christianity flourished more in Northern Ireland than anywhere else in the world. The people of Northern Ireland were called Celts, and they produced a musical sound that is still with us today. The worship songs of the Celtic Christians have since been translated into many languages but have retained much of the emotion and sincerity of the Irish Christians who wrote them. The place: Ireland. The year: 750.

Have the band begin to play "Be Thou My Vision" as a female vocalist sings the first verse.

14C *Display the lyrics on the screen, and invite everyone to sing.*

Slide 3: The Latin Period

Display the photo "Italy 1265" on the screen.

Narrator: As new people groups migrated through Europe in the 13th century, the people and languages began to change rapidly. To unify Christians in their worship celebrations throughout the world, the church offered one "worship language." The language was Latin, and Christians throughout Europe used it to celebrate the presence of God.

However, since most people couldn't speak Latin, most of the words in their worship services meant little to the average person wanting to celebrate God. The solution the church employed was to create simple songs with only a few key words in Latin that people had to learn. These songs were sung in church every time people gathered.

The "Kyrie" is one of those songs. The song has only three Latin words. The first phrase is "Kyrie eleison," which means "Lord have mercy." The second phrase is "Christe eleison," meaning "Christ have mercy." The place: Italy. The year: 1265.

Have the band begin to play ethereal sounds as a soloist sings the "Kyrie." You may want to have your band do this as a performance piece. Or, if your church is used to songs like this, ask the congregation to join in singing.

Slide 4: The Reformation

Display the photo "Germany 1529" on the screen.

Narrator: At the end of the Dark Ages and the beginning of the Enlightenment, many church leaders began to stress the need for a more cognitive, rational experience of God. They sought to better understand God and how he affects the world around us.

One of the great religious leaders of the time was Martin Luther. Luther wrote worship songs in the language of the people rather than in Latin. He translated the Bible into German and wrote Bible commentaries and hymn books in the language of his people. Here is Martin Luther's most famous hymn, based on Psalm 46. The place: Germany. The year: 1529.

14D *Display the lyrics of "A Mighty Fortress Is Our God" on the screen. Have the keyboardist begin to play the song using a giant full-pipes organ sound. Invite everyone to stand and sing.*

Slide 5: The African-American Spiritual Period
Display the photo "Alabama 1862" on the screen.

Narrator: Many people believe that jazz was the first musical style indigenous to the United States. In reality, jazz was derived from the Christian spirituals that sustained American slaves through the hardships they endured in the 19th century.

Slaves identified with the message of Jesus' suffering—and his promise of redemption and salvation. The promise of better days in heaven gave them the hope they longed for.

Those experiencing the torment of slavery saw in the person of Jesus someone with whom they could feel intimately connected. The place: Alabama. The year: 1862.

14E *Display the lyrics of "Were You There" on the screen. As the keyboardist begins to play, have a single vocalist—perhaps an African American—enter and begin to sing. After the first verse, have the worship leader invite everyone to sing.*

Slide 6: Gospel Period
Display the photo "Tennessee 1932" on the screen.

Narrator: Another form of music that had a huge impact on Christian worship in the United States is called, simply, gospel. Gospel music laid the groundwork for much of today's worship music. It's still a major worship format for millions of Christians all over the United States.

Songs that typify that period are characterized by short, repetitive phrases accompanied by much movement and excitement. One such song is "I'll Fly Away." Gospel is a great example of Christians celebrating Christ and his message in a style and way that makes sense to them. The place: Tennessee. The year: 1932.

Have the band kick into a fun, foot-stomping version of "I'll Fly Away" by Albert E. Brumley. Then invite everyone to sing along.

Slide 7: The 1980s

Display the photo "Colorado 1988" on the screen.

Narrator: In the early 1980s, Christian songwriters began to use words and melodies from the present instead of phrases and sounds from the past. Generally these songs were focused on worship and celebration.

One such song was written by Rich Mullins as he was driving through the mountains of Colorado. When traffic slowed to a crawl, Rich had time to look around and was struck by the beauty of God's awesome creation. The place: Colorado. The year: 1988.

Have the band begin to play "Awesome God" by Rich Mullins, and invite everyone to sing.

Slide 8: The 1990s

Display the photo "Ontario, Canada 1996" on the screen.

Narrator: In the 1990s, worship music changed again, reflecting world and church events. New centers of worship influence arose in places such as California and Canada. Christian songs began to speak more about the human condition, our shortcomings, and whom we should follow. The place: Ontario, Canada. The year: 1996.

Have the worship leader and band lead the congregation in singing "You're Worthy of My Praise" by David Ruis.

Slide 9: The 2000s

Display an image of your community and the current year on the screen.

Narrator: And now we arrive at the 21st century. Worship is again transforming itself, engaging all the senses with a new focus—intimacy. The songs of the first decade of the third millennium often speak of knowing God more intimately and

giving ourselves to God. The place: here. The year: now.
Lead the congregation in singing "Surrender" by Marc James.

Closing

Point out the artists' completed works, and invite everyone to come forward at the end of the service to view them and talk to the artists about their themes.

Prayer

Pastor: Lord, we worship you now, just as your children have for thousands of years. The day will come when we will gather at your feet in heaven with every person who has called on your name throughout all of history. And we will worship you with one voice. Lord, hear our cries. Hear our joy. And, Lord, hear our celebration of your name. Amen.

Worship Blueprint 15

Made Special

Theme
Letting God use us to create a unique community

Goal
To encourage people to rejoice in their uniqueness and the special way they fit into the community

Scripture
Ephesians 2:10

SUMMARY OF THE EXPERIENCE

Mood: exploratory and celebratory

Synopsis: Through a movie clip, poetry, short talks, and music, you'll set up two interactive experiences that lead people to think about being made special by God. These elements are woven through the service so it flows seamlessly.

The first experience focuses on the individual and the fact that each person is made to be unique. Clay is distributed at the door; then participants are asked to place their thumbprints in the clay and reflect on their own unique qualities.

In the second experience, everyone helps create a mosaic, demonstrating that each individual is a part of a community that

For we are God's workmanship, created in Christ Jesus to do good works, which God prepared in advance for us to do.
—Ephesians 2:10

can accomplish bigger things for God than individuals can by themselves.

The experience concludes with Communion.

What people will

see: their thumbprints in clay, the outline of a mosaic, a finished mosaic

taste: the elements of the Lord's Supper

touch: clay, individual mosaic pieces

do: make thumbprints in clay, contribute to a mosaic

CREATING AN ENVIRONMENT FOR WORSHIP

Simple Environment

Set up a mosaic on the floor by outlining a design with masking tape. Use broken pieces of tile, torn paper, or stones that have been spray-painted different colors.

Recruit someone from your congregation to recite or read a poem about God's design for each person's uniqueness.

If your tradition permits congregants to serve themselves Communion, set out the elements on a table (or on several tables if your group is large) covered with a tablecloth. Place several candles on the table.

Hand out lumps of clay as people enter the worship area.

Play upbeat music as people enter and leave the worship area and quiet, contemplative music during the service.

Supplies for a Simple Environment

- *Pleasantville* movie clip and the appropriate license for showing it (Cue the movie to 1:42:03, the scene that opens with "Bud Parker. William Johnson." End the clip at 1:46:27, after David [Bud] says, "And you can't stop something that's inside you.") In this clip, David and Bill are formally charged with "desecrating a public building" with a colorful mural.
- material with which to make a mosaic—pieces of stained glass, pieces of broken tile, stones, or torn paper, for example
- modeling clay
- person to perform a piece of original poetry or recite a conventional poem
- Communion elements
- tables
- tablecloths
- candles

Maximum Environment

This is a good chance to unleash the creativity of the artists in your church. If you decide to use stained glass for the mosaic, the project will be more expensive and time-consuming, but the end result will be beautiful. Utilize the expertise of one or two people who have taken a stained-glass class and know how to cut and sand the glass. Place an adhesive magnetic strip (available at home-improvement stores) on the back of each piece of stained glass. Arrange the stained glass pieces by their colors in baskets or metal containers that coordinate with the rest of your props. You'll also need a large metal board that magnets will stick to. Use thin black tape to make a design on the board, and label each area with the color of stained glass that will be placed in it. Set the containers of stained glass near the board.

If your congregation includes a poet, recruit that person to perform a piece on God's special design for each person to be unique.

If your tradition allows congregants to serve themselves Communion, set up several tables in the middle of the room. Cover the tables with black fabric; then place all the Communion elements on the tables. Display the elements in a variety of containers such as plates, bowls, and glasses.

Place a small amount of modeling clay inside individual containers. You can purchase metal tins with lids from www .specialtybottle.com. (You'll need one container for each participant.)

Just inside the doors, place two large metal containers, such as fire pits or metal buckets. Place the tins of clay in these containers, and have volunteers stand at the doors and hand out the tins as people enter.

To soften the room's lighting, place large glass vases with candles in them around the room.

To create a totally different environment from the one people are used to, remove the chairs from the worship space and encourage people to sit on the floor. Place the mosaic board on the floor, and use low tables for Communion. Leave some chairs around the perimeter of the room for people who might have trouble sitting on the floor.

Play upbeat music as people enter and leave the worship area and quiet, contemplative music during the service.

Additional Supplies for Maximizing the Experience

- stained glass
- volunteers to cut and sand stained glass
- adhesive magnetic strips
- baskets or metal containers
- large metal board
- thin black tape
- low tables for Communion
- black fabric
- plates, bowls, and glasses for Communion table
- tin containers for modeling clay (you'll need 1 for each participant)
- 2 metal fire pits or buckets
- large glass vases
- large candles

The Experience

Song Set 1
- "Here I Am to Worship" by Tim Hughes
- "Not to Us" by Chris Tomlin and Jesse Reeves
- "Everything" by Chris Tomlin and Jesse Reeves

Pleasantville Movie Clip
Show the clip.

Clay Prints
Discuss the idea that God has designed each of us to be unique. After ensuring that everyone has been given modeling clay, ask participants to press their thumbs into the clay. Encourage them to examine their thumbprints and consider their uniqueness. Describe how each person makes a distinctive imprint on the world.

If someone in your congregation is a poet, invite him or her to perform an original piece. Alternatively, have someone read or recite a fitting poem about God's design for our uniqueness.

Communion
Explain your church's approach to the Lord's Supper, and invite worshippers to partake.

Play soft music as people take part in Communion. If you have a band that's able to create music on the fly, this would be a great time for the band to improvise, demonstrating how a group made of up of unique individuals can come together as a community to create beautiful music. Allow the worship music to continue for several minutes after everyone has taken part in Communion.

Mosaic Masterpiece

Explain that the individuals gathered in your worship space fit into your church community like pieces of a mosaic. They are various shapes, sizes, and colors, and when they come together, they create a beautiful piece of art.

Invite everyone to come forward, take a piece of whatever material you've chosen for the mosaic, and place it in the designated space. As worshippers complete the mosaic, have the band or a CD play "The Reason" by Doug Robb. Allow several minutes for people to contribute to the mosaic and to admire the finished product.

Song Set 2
- "Worth It All" by Rita Springer
- "Blessed Be Your Name" by Matt Redman and Beth Redman

Closing

Pull together the whole service by emphasizing the uniqueness of individuals and the beautiful thing God makes of groups of individuals when they work together.

Worship Blueprint 16

Reflection

Theme

Thinking of ourselves as children of God

Goal

To help people see themselves as God sees them and to remove some of the artificial barriers people place between themselves and God

Scriptures

2 Corinthians 5:17; Colossians 1:21-22

SUMMARY OF THE EXPERIENCE

Mood: reflective

Synopsis: This service encourages people to consider how God sees them in spite of all they've done to separate themselves from him. Upon entering the worship area, everyone is given a small square of rice paper and a pencil. Each square has a picture of a mirror stamped on it. During the message, the pastor challenges listeners to write on the rice paper the misconceptions that prevent them from seeing themselves as God does.

People are then asked to approach a basin of moving water and place the rice paper in the water. They'll watch as the writing

Therefore, if anyone is in Christ, he is a new creation; the old has gone, the new has come!

—*2 Corinthians 5:17*

and then the entire paper dissolve, symbolically carrying away their regrets and sins.

What people will

see: video images of water, symbols of the sin and hurt in their lives dissolving in water

hear: sounds of falling water and songs about cleansing

touch: rice paper

CREATING AN ENVIRONMENT FOR WORSHIP

Simple Environment

Place a large container, such as a metal washtub, at the front of the worship area, and place an aquarium bubbler in it. (Aquarium bubblers are available at pet stores.) Fill the container with water.

Purchase rice paper from a magician supply store or the Internet, being sure to buy the kind that dissolves in water. Cut the sheets of rice paper into squares or rectangles. (An 8½x11-inch sheet of rice paper will yield nine decent-sized rectangles.)

Purchase a stamp of a mirror and a red ink pad at a craft store or scrapbooking store. The stamp can depict an elaborate mirror or a simple oval shape. Stamp a mirror on each piece of rice paper.

Supplies for a Simple Environment
- rice paper
- pencils
- stamp of a mirror
- red ink pad
- basin of water
- aquarium bubbler
- CD-ROM:
  "Blueprint 16" folder:
  - 16A, "Rippling Water" video
  - 16B, "Come, Thou Fount" lyrics (optional)
  - 16C, "I Surrender All" lyrics (optional)
  - 16D, "Amazing Grace" lyrics (optional)

Maximum Environment

Set up several large fountains at the front of the worship area. Make sure the fountains remain on during the entire service to reinforce the idea of cleansing water. One option is to use large plastic flowerpots (at least 15 inches in diameter) with a "flowerpot fountain" in each one. These are self-contained, recirculating fountains that create an impressive and continuous movement of water. They are available on the Internet or through home-and-garden stores.

Purchase rice paper from a magician supply store or the Internet, being sure to buy the kind that dissolves in water. Cut the sheets of rice paper into squares or rectangles. (An 8½x11-inch sheet of rice paper will yield nine decent-sized rectangles.)

Purchase a stamp of a mirror and a red ink pad at a craft store or scrapbooking store. The stamp can depict an elaborate mirror or a simple oval shape. Stamp a mirror on each piece of rice paper.

Recruit a gifted actor from your congregation to be videotaped playing the role of a woman undergoing a reality TV–type makeover. Make sure the approach is serious and is *not* a parody. Videotape two scenes. In the first, have the woman appear with unkempt hair, and without makeup. Her demeanor should convey that she is full of self-loathing because of her appearance. In this "before" interview, have her describe how she hates her

appearance, how she was teased as a child, and how desperately she longs to be accepted. In the second, "after" interview, have her appear fully made up and well coifed. Her attitude should be exuberant as she discusses how thrilled she is with her new look. End the interview with a shot of her preening in the mirror.

Additional Supplies for Maximizing the Experience
- several large fountains
- videographer
- video equipment
- actor to play the role of a person who undergoes a makeover

THE EXPERIENCE

Opening

As people arrive, give each person a piece of rice paper and a pencil.

Makeover Video (optional)

Open the experience by showing the video of the woman undergoing a makeover.

Message

Consider using any of the following points in the message:
- Self-esteem is really about how much we like ourselves.

- Most of us know that God loves us, but very few of us believe that God genuinely *likes* us. But he does.
- God has shown his love for us and his opinion of our worth by creating us, forgiving us, and continually renewing us.
- We often create artificial barriers that separate us from God.
- God wants us to see ourselves as he sees us, unblemished and free from accusation (Colossians 1:21-22).

The Forgiveness Experience

Have the pastor read the following text or use it as a springboard for the message.

Pastor: We often seek our identities and our sense of worth in things other than the simple fact that God made us. When we do this, we face all sorts of unintended consequences. For example, when we identify ourselves with what we do for a living, work can turn into workaholism. We can end up worshipping work or the money or accolades that it brings because we think that work determines our worth.

Sometimes we identify ourselves by our relationships. When we use relationships to prove our worth, we tend to treat people as objects. And real love is replaced by approval seeking, as we use people and let people use us to gain the acceptance everyone craves.

So often we define ourselves by our appearance. We might feel too fat, too thin, too short, or too tall. Our hair may be too straight or too curly, too thick or not at all. Our skin may be too pale or too dark, too freckled or too blemished. When we concentrate on our perceived physical flaws, we turn inward and can become full of self-loathing. On the other hand, when we are enthralled by our own physical beauty, we can become self-centered and fearful of losing that beauty.

How do you define yourself? How do you measure your worth? Do your identity and the measurements you use to evaluate your worth cloud your idea of God's perception of you? Does this place a barrier between you and God?

Dare to be really honest with yourself for the next few minutes. On the piece of paper you've been given, write words or draw pictures or symbols inside the mirror shape that represent the ways you identify yourself that create a barrier between yourself and God. You might write the word *job* or draw a picture of a paycheck. You might write the word *lifestyle* if you gauge your value and significance by your standard of living. You might write the word *education* if you feel that the degree you've earned or hope to earn will prove your worth or significance. You might write the word *marriage* or *boyfriend* or *girlfriend* if you realize that you view romantic relationships as a reflection of who you really are. Or maybe you'll write *children* because being a parent is your proof that you're worthwhile. Maybe you'll write the word *body* or *attractiveness* because you feel your appearance equates with your worth.

This is not about what you enjoy; it's about those things that you think define you. Take this time right now to identify those things you use to tell you whether you matter, whether others should like you, and whether you should like yourself.

In a few moments, you'll have an opportunity to come to the front of the worship area and place your mirror—filled with doubts, hurts, and barriers—in cleansing water.

"Rippling Water" Video and Song Set

16A As people write on their rice paper, play the "Rippling Water" video on the CD-ROM and as many of the following songs as you'd like:
- "Give Us Clean Hands" by Charlie Hall
16B • "Come, Thou Fount" by Robert Robinson
- "Your Love, Oh Lord" by Brad Avery, David Carr, Johnny Mac Powell, Mark D. Lee, and Tai Anderson
16C • "I Surrender All" by Judson W. Van de Venter
- "Find Me in the River" by Martin Smith
- "At the Cross" by Randy Butler and Terry Butler
- "Consuming Fire" by Tim Hughes
- "Grace Flows Down" by David E. Bell, Louie Giglio, and Rod Padgett
16D • "Amazing Grace" by John Newton

The Cleansing

After your time of worship in music, continue to play the "Rippling Water" video on the CD-ROM as people come forward and place their slips of rice paper in the water. As people approach the water, they'll see that the water is flowing. It's very important that the water is moving to symbolize the living water of Jesus Christ. Still water is also less effective in dissolving the paper.

When people place their papers in the water, they'll first see the ink of the stamp begin to run, and soon the mirror will be gone. The water will begin to turn red, symbolizing the cleansing blood of Christ. Soon the paper will begin to dissolve and eventually will completely disappear. Encourage people to stay quietly at the water until their papers are completely gone.

(Experiment with this in advance to find the best setup for your church's environment. The water's temperature and the strength of the fountain determine how long the process will take.)

Continue until the entire community finishes the process.

Conclusion

Remind listeners that the barriers we've erected between ourselves and God will be dissolved if we recognize them and relinquish them.

Worship Blueprint 17

Remembering

Theme

Taking time to remember what Jesus experienced as he prepared to face death on the cross (This service works well on Palm Sunday, in preparation for Easter.)

Goal

To reflect on Jesus' sacrifice and the pain he endured

Scripture

Luke 22

SUMMARY OF THE EXPERIENCE

Mood: reflective

Synopsis: This experience involves minimal speaking from the platform. Other elements are used instead, such as a Scripture reading, a movie clip, reflection while music is played, small-group discussions, journaling, and Communion. As people arrive, the most noticeable change to the worship area is a long table set as if for the Last Supper. Communion elements are served from the table. People are encouraged to take plentifully from the table as if they are taking part in a meal, as the disciples were during the Last Supper.

*And he took bread,
gave thanks and broke
it, and gave it to them,
saying, "This is my body
given for you; do this in
remembrance of me."*
—*Luke 22:19*

What people will

see: candlelight, a long table set as for the Last Supper, a movie clip

hear: poetry, Scripture readings, music

taste: Communion elements

do: reflect, journal, take Communion

CREATING AN ENVIRONMENT FOR WORSHIP

Simple Environment

Place one 8-foot table at the front of the room. Cover it with a tablecloth, and set out the Communion elements. In addition, pile grapes and cheese on platters. Make the table look full and inviting. Set the table as it might have been set for the Last Supper, using pieces of rustic crockery. Set out small glasses and plates as well to make it look like a table set for a meal. Lower the room's ambient lighting, and place several pillar candles on the table.

Supplies for a Simple Environment
- long table or tables
- long tablecloth
- Communion elements
- platters overflowing with cheese and grapes
- rustic plates and cups
- candles

- person to read a poem or hymn about Jesus' sacrifice on the cross
- *Jesus* (the movie from 1979) clip and the appropriate license for showing it (Cue the movie to 48:05, when the camera zooms in on Jesus and the disciples sitting around a table. End it at 51:22, at the end of the scene, after Jesus tells Peter he will deny Jesus three times.)
- paper
- pens or pencils

Maximum Environment

Place several long tables together, end to end, and set them lengthwise in the middle of the worship area. The long table should be the focal point of the room and should immediately catch the attention of everyone entering. Cover the table with a roughly woven fabric. Set the table as if for dinner, using earthy crockery that looks like it could have been used during Jesus' time. Place napkins, small cups, and stacks of small plates on the table intermittently around the place settings. Then fill the table with Communion elements, using chunks of French bread. In addition, pile grapes and cheese on platters. Make the table look full and inviting. Lower the room's ambient lighting, and place pillar candles along the middle of the long table.

Additional Supplies for Maximizing the Experience
- roughly woven fabric

The Experience

As people arrive, give everyone a sheet of paper and a pen or pencil, or place these items on each seat before people arrive.

Song Set 1

- "Take Us In" by Dan Wilt and Bruce Ellis
- "Blessed Be Your Name" by Matt Redman and Beth Redman

Poetry Reading

Have someone read poetry related to Jesus' sacrificial death. A thoughtful reading of a hymn such as "At the Cross," "The Old Rugged Cross," "When I Survey the Wondrous Cross," or "There Is a Green Hill Far Away" would also work well.

Scripture Reading

Have someone read aloud Luke 22:7-38 from *The Message.*

Message

Consider using any of the following points in the message:

- Jesus knew that he was facing the cross as he sat down for a final meal with his disciples.
- This meal was not what we think of when we think of Communion. It was an evening meal, and the disciples ate for sustenance.
- The departure of Judas probably put a damper on things, but no one except Jesus and Judas knew what it really meant.
- After this meal Jesus would not eat again. He died almost 24 hours later.
- We partake of Communion to remember Jesus' broken body and shed blood, which were given freely so we might have eternal life through faith in him.

Communion

Have the pastor explain your church's approach to Communion. If your tradition allows, encourage people to come forward and fill their plates as if they are eating that last meal with Jesus. As they eat and drink, encourage them to think about Jesus' sacrifice.

Play soft music as people fill their plates and eat.

Jesus Movie Clip

Set up the clip by explaining that it depicts what Scripture tells us was said at the Last Supper. It is a good visual reminder of what Jesus experienced that night and is a great setup for the following group discussion.

Group Discussion

Have people form groups of four or five and discuss the following questions:
- If you had been a disciple at the Last Supper and knew only what the disciples knew at the time, what do you think you would have said to Jesus during that meal?
- What do you think you would have been pondering as you came away from that meal?

Featured Song

"Have a Little Faith in Me" by John Hiatt

Journaling

Consider using any of the following points in this part of the message:
- Imagine what it would have been like to stand at the foot of the cross and watch Jesus die.
- Think about what Jesus' death has done for humanity in general. What if Jesus had not come to earth?
- What would your life be like without Jesus? What if you didn't know him?
- How do you think Jesus feels when we ignore his sacrifice for us?

Have the pastor encourage listeners to consider these questions carefully and then write down their responses. Play quiet, reflective music as people think and record their thoughts. Allow as long as 10 minutes for people to carefully consider the questions they've been asked.

Song Set 2
- "Surrender" by Marc James
- "Draw Me Close" by Kelly Carpenter

Featured Song
"You Are So Beautiful" by Billy Preston and Bruce Fisher

Conclusion
Have your pastor close this worship time with prayer.

Worship Blueprint 18

Redeemed

Theme

Letting God take us as we are and turn us into something beautiful

Goal

To help people see that God is a redeemer who wants to bring us into a relationship with him

Scriptures

Romans 3:22-24; 1 Corinthians 1:27-30

SUMMARY OF THE EXPERIENCE

Mood: upbeat

Synopsis: Each individual will be given a small, sealed envelope containing a coffee bean. At a certain point in the service, people will be asked to open their envelopes and examine the contents. The pastor will then tell them the story behind these very expensive beans, and this will lead into a discussion of the idea that God can truly take *anything* and make it valuable.

After the service, anyone who is interested will be given a sample of brewed coffee.

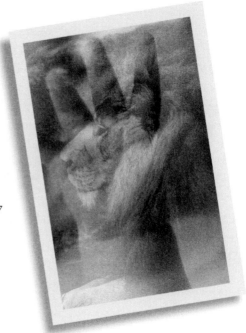

But God chose the foolish things of the world to shame the wise; God chose the weak things of the world to shame the strong.
—1 Corinthians 1:27

What people will

smell: a coffee bean and brewed coffee

touch: a coffee bean

taste: coffee

CREATING AN ENVIRONMENT FOR WORSHIP

Simple Environment

Place one Kopi Luwak coffee bean in a small envelope for each person in your congregation. Seal the envelopes.

Serve regular coffee after the service.

Supplies for a Simple Environment

- 1 Kopi Luwak coffee bean for each worshipper
- small envelopes
- coffee
- coffee makers
- coffee cups
- CD-ROM:
  "Blueprint 18" folder:
  - 18A, "Be Thou My Vision" lyrics (optional)
  - 18B, "Amazing Grace" lyrics (optional)
  - 18C, "Holy, Holy, Holy" lyrics (optional)

Maximum Environment

Purchase Kopi Luwak coffee from a coffee merchant on the Internet. Kopi Luwak is reputed to be the rarest, most expensive coffee in the world and, at this printing, costs about $75 per quarter-pound. Calculate the amount of coffee you will need based on giving very small samples (about one ounce each) to the people in your congregation who may be willing to taste the coffee after they know its unique origins.

Place one Kopi Luwak coffee bean in a small envelope for each person in your congregation. Seal the envelopes.

Set up a large area for drinking coffee and interacting after the service. You might even want to transform the worship area into a coffeehouse and serve small samples of the Kopi Luwak there after the service.

Additional Supplies for Maximizing the Experience

- enough Kopi Luwak coffee to give everyone a small sample
- small tables and chairs

THE EXPERIENCE

Opening

As people enter, make sure everyone is given an envelope with a single coffee bean in it. Play upbeat, friendly music.

Song Set 1

Choose as many of the following as you'd like:
- "Refiner's Fire" by Brian Doerksen
- "Beautiful One" by Tim Hughes
- "40" by Bono (U2)
- "Give Us Clean Hands" by Charlie Hall
- "Kindness" by Chris Tomlin, Jesse Reeves, and Louie Giglio
- "Salvation" by Charlie Hall

A Redemption Story

After the congregation has been seated and the music has ended, have the pastor tell the following story or use it as a springboard for the message.

Pastor: Go ahead and open your envelope. A coffee bean! Take that coffee bean and smell it. Any coffee connoisseurs here? Feel free to put it in your mouth and taste it. You can do whatever you want with it, but what you have in your hand is absolutely the most expensive coffee bean in the world.

Pause to allow people to examine the coffee beans, then continue:

This type of coffee is extremely rare. It comes from only one part of the planet, a part of the world known for its great coffee, Indonesia.

Some coffee connoisseurs consider this the most exquisite, exotic, complex-tasting coffee in the world. Let me ask coffee lovers: How much does a pound of really great roasted coffee beans cost? *(Wait for answers.)* Well, this stuff costs $300 or more a pound! This coffee is so expensive that it's sold by the ounce—the only coffee that's sold in such a small increment. That's what you have in your hand.

It is called Kopi Luwak.

This coffee has a very interesting story. *Kopi* is an Indonesian word for coffee. A *luwak* is a jungle cat. It's about the size of a fox and is active only at night. The luwak has one very unusual habit. In fact, this cat is the Juan Valdez of the animal kingdom. It picks only the ripest, reddest coffee cherries and eats them. After eating them, the cat digests them. The coffee bean actually emerges from the digestive process fairly intact. The enzymes in the animal's

stomach apparently add something unique to the bean's flavor, and growers have learned to harvest these beans for their unique, rich flavor. So the coffee bean you're holding in your hand has been harvested from…well, you get the picture!

Wait for responses.

Every single one of the beans you're holding has passed through the digestive tract of an Indonesian wildcat. These beans cost $300 a pound.

Now remember, with God a lot of good things come out of unlikely places. Listen to 1 Corinthians 1:27-30: "God chose the foolish things of the world to shame the wise; God chose the weak things of the world to shame the strong. He chose the lowly things of this world and the despised things—and the things that are not—to nullify the things that are, so that no one may boast before him. It is because of him that you are in Christ Jesus, who has become for us wisdom from God—that is, our righteousness, holiness, and redemption."

Message

Consider using any of the following points in the message:
- God can "recycle" even the most useless and dirty things into tools that are invaluable in his plan.
- No matter what we've done, what "manure" we've been in, God loves us.
- No matter what we've done, God can redeem us.
- God uses people who've been through a lot of bad things, and he can use you!

Song Set 2

Play as many of the following as you'd like:
- "Let the Redeemed" by John Barnett
- "I Will Never Be" by Geoff Bullock
- "I Will Offer Up My Life" by Matt Redman
- **18A** • "Be Thou My Vision" translated by Mary Byrne
- **18B** • "Amazing Grace" by John Newton
- **18C** • "Holy, Holy, Holy" by Reginald Heber

Coffee Is Served

Close the service by challenging people to turn their lives over to Jesus to be used in serving him.

Encourage people to take their coffee beans home and put them in a place where they'll see them often, reminding them of what God can do in their lives. Invite everyone to try a small taste of this mysterious and expensive coffee.

Worship Blueprint 19

Spoken Word Worship

Theme

Praising God through poetry created by the congregation

Goal

To give people a chance to voice their praise in a creative way and share with each other the struggles and joys of Christian life

Scriptures

Psalm 65; Psalm 73:21-28; Psalm 89:1-18; Psalm 96:1-6

SUMMARY OF THE EXPERIENCE

Mood: upbeat and celebratory

Synopsis: This is basically an open-mic service revolving around praising God through poetry. Several weeks before the event, worshippers are encouraged to "sing a new song to the Lord" by either composing their own poems or thinking of existing poems they would like to read to the congregation. The week before the actual worship service, the readings are previewed and placed in the context of the entire service. During the service, these readings are interspersed with songs, Scripture readings, and famous poems. Finally, everyone is encouraged to write a haiku praising God and to share it in a group of four or five. The haikus

Sing to the Lord, praise his name; proclaim his salvation day after day.
—Psalm 96:2

from each group are then linked together to create a longer poem, and some are then read to the entire congregation.

What people will

> *see:* "Praise as Poetry" video

> *hear:* poems read by their fellow worshippers

> *do:* compose their own original poems and then combine them with the poems of others to create a new work of art

CREATING AN ENVIRONMENT FOR WORSHIP

Simple Environment

Place a stool, a music stand, and a microphone on the platform. Dim the lights, and aim a spotlight at the stool and microphone. Have the spotlight on as people arrive so it is the focal point of the room.

Supplies for a Simple Environment

- CD-ROM:
  "Blueprint 19" folder:
    - 19A, "Haiku Instructions"
    - 19B, "Miracles" by Walt Whitman
    - 19C, "Praise as Poetry" video

- *Facedown* DVD by Matt Redman (optional)
- volunteers to read 3 or 4 famous poems
- 4 volunteers to read Psalm 65; Psalm 73:21-28; Psalm 89:1-18; and Psalm 96:1-6 from *The Message*
- index cards (1 for each person in the congregation)
- pens or pencils
- tape (at least 1 roll of tape for every 15 people)
- copies of your order of worship so all presenters know when they are supposed to present
- volunteers to distribute "Haiku Instructions," index cards, pens or pencils, and tape

Maximum Environment

Set up the worship area to resemble a coffeehouse, complete with coffee. It should feel like an inviting place to share one's feelings about God. Set up round tables and chairs. Place a drippy candle on each table, and turn the lights down low. On the stage set up a stool, a music stand, and a microphone. Aim a spotlight at the stool and microphone, and have the spotlight on as people arrive so it is the focal point of the room.

Additional Supplies for Maximizing the Experience
- coffee
- coffee cups
- coffeemakers
- volunteers to serve coffee
- small tables and chairs
- candles

The Experience

Preparing for the Event

One Month Before the Event

Begin to announce the upcoming "Spoken Word Worship" gathering, and encourage people to compose poetry praising God or to think of existing poems they would like to share at the event.

19B Find two or three famous poems praising God, and plan to use them in the worship service along with "Miracles" by Walt Whitman.

Three Weeks Before the Event

If you have access to the *Facedown* DVD by Matt Redman, play the poem "Spoken Word Worship" by Amena Brown. Try to use it as part of your worship service, not just as an announcement. This is a great example of how performance poetry can be used in worship.

Two Weeks Before the Event

Enlist volunteers to present the famous poems you've chosen. Ask them to spend time preparing their presentations. In addition, enlist volunteers to present Psalm 65; Psalm 73:21-28; Psalm 89:1-18; and Psalm 96:1-6 from *The Message*. These will be used between songs and during the service.

Announce a time for people to present their poems to you for screening. The purpose of this screening isn't to weed out inferior poems; it is to allow you to organize the service.

The Week of the Event

List the poetry readers in the order they will read during the service. You may want to group similar ideas or similar styles. Be flexible and allow the Holy Spirit to guide you as you create this order. If possible, call the presenters during the week to pray with them and encourage them.

The Day Before the Event

Give everyone who will be participating on the platform during the service a written outline of the service; then rehearse the entire service with everyone who will be taking part.

19A Make enough copies of the "Haiku Instructions" for everyone to have one.

Song and Psalm Set 1

- "Not to Us" by Jesse Reeves and Chris Tomlin
- Reading: Psalm 96:1-6
- "Hallelujah (Your Love Is Amazing)" by Brenton Brown and Brian Doerksen
- Reading: Psalm 65
- "May the Words of My Mouth" by Tim Hughes and Rob Hill

Welcome

Pastor: We're here to praise God. He's great and mighty and worthy of all our praise. He has given us the ability to praise his name. Today we come to use that gift to honor him with our words. This isn't about church words or fancy speeches. This is about the words of our hearts, lifted in praise to the almighty God. Step up and speak the truth God has laid on your heart. Step up to the microphone, speak your praise, and let us all worship together.

"Praise as Poetry" Video

19C Play the "Praise as Poetry" video.

Poetry Set

Instruct the first reader to begin as the video presentation ends, and each person to follow in order. Remind presenters to keep their extra speaking to a minimum and to let the poetry speak for itself. As the poetry readers come forward one at a time, there is no need to introduce them. This is about praising God, not individuals. Blend in a couple of the famous poems where they are most appropriate. This poetry set should last 15 to 20 minutes or until there is a natural break.

Haiku Praise

This is a chance to encourage everyone to sing a new praise to God by writing haiku poetry. It's an important part of the worship service because it moves people beyond observing to participating in a creative act of praise.

19A Distribute index cards, pens or pencils, and the "Haiku Instructions" to everyone. Invite people to write their own haikus praising God.

To help reduce distractions, play soft instrumental music as people are writing. After everyone has had a chance to create a haiku, have the congregation form groups of five (10 to 12 if your congregation is large). Ask them to share their haikus with one another and then, as volunteers distribute tape, to put their haikus together to read as one long poem. Tell them to decide on the best order for the poems and to then tape them together in that order. Finally, ask them to choose one person from each group to come forward and present the group's combined poem to the entire congregation.

If you're pressed for time, have just two or three groups share their poems. Explain that the other groups' poems will be used in later worship settings. (After the readings, be sure to gather all the poem chains and find a way to use them in later worship settings.)

Song and Psalm Set 2

- "Here I Am to Worship" by Tim Hughes
- Reading: Psalm 73:21-28
- "The Heart of Worship" by Matt Redman
- Reading: Psalm 89:1-18

Response

Poetry is a powerful worship tool, and hearing the heartfelt worship of others can be enlightening and moving. Include a time for people to respond to the praise they've witnessed. You might want to sing an additional song and invite people to come forward to pray or have paper and pens available so they can write about their feelings. After a song, if people are still writing or praying, ask everyone else to leave quietly and allow those who are still worshipping to continue. Play soft music as people leave.

Worship Blueprint 20

What God Wants

Theme

Deepening our relationships with God

Goal

To help people realize that God is pursuing us to deepen our relationships with him

Scripture

John 5:17

SUMMARY OF THE EXPERIENCE

Mood: upbeat

Synopsis: The first half of this experience centers on a large screen in the front of the worship area where the image of an offstage computer screen is projected. People enter the worship area to find a "chat room" conversation between "God" and the congregation taking place on the screen. "God" asks several questions and waits for people to respond. He even comments on what people in the room are doing. "God" then begins to probe the people about their relationships with him.

After 10 to 15 minutes of the chat-room dialogue, the pastor delivers the message; then people partake of Communion. During Communion "God" appears on Instant Messenger and

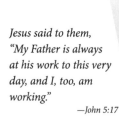

*Jesus said to them,
"My Father is always
at his work to this very
day, and I, too, am
working."*
—John 5:17

tells the congregation that he loves them and that he sent his Son for them.

The service ends with a special time of worship through music. A solitary worship leader with a guitar sits on a stool in the middle of the crowd and leads the audience in singing songs of love to God, a one-on-one conversation.

What people will

see: a chat-room conversation with "God," instant-messages from "God"

hear: worship songs accompanied by a single acoustic guitar

taste: Communion elements

do: speak out loud during the chat-room conversation, have a "worship conversation" with God through singing

CREATING AN ENVIRONMENT FOR WORSHIP

Simple Environment

Connect two computers to the Internet, and set up a private chat-room link. Create and register two screen names: one for God and one for the congregation. Project the chat-room conversation onto a large screen in the worship area.

The success of this idea depends on the sensitivity, verbal aptitude, and timing of the people who are offstage creating the chat-room conversation. Be sure to select people whose understanding of biblical truth will guide them in choosing appropriate words and topics throughout the conversation. If necessary, create much of the dialogue beforehand, and give it to the computer operators to type in during the service.

Ask a few people who will be in the congregation to be prepared to answer God's questions out loud. This will prompt others to answer spontaneously.

For the last part of the experience, set up a stool in the midst of the crowd, taking the focus off the stage and removing any distractions that would prevent people from worshipping God. If it's possible to darken the worship area sufficiently, shine a solitary light on the worship leader in an otherwise dark room to produce this focused atmosphere.

Supplies for a Simple Environment

- 2 computers offstage, connected to the Internet and able to be projected onto a screen in your worship area
- 2 computer operators offstage
- Communion elements
- worship leader playing an acoustic guitar

Maximum Environment

To maximize the visual effect of this experience, stack several computer monitors on each side of the stage and ensure that they have the same video signal traveling to them as the one that's traveling to the large screen. Stack the monitors so some are right side up and some are turned sideways. Project other images of computer chat-room conversations with God on other screens.

Additional Supplies for Maximizing the Experience

- several additional computer monitors
- images of chat-room dialogues

THE EXPERIENCE

God's Chat Room

As people enter the worship space, they'll see a large screen that contains a chat-room conversation, accompanied by quiet, ethereal music. The conversation appears to be taking place

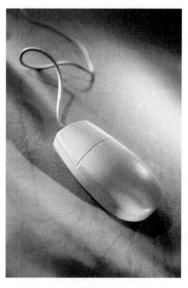

between the congregation and God. God is identified by his screen name, "God_1" (or something similar). God is trying to have a conversation with the congregation.

As the experience continues, have the person creating God's part of the conversation begin to try to get the congregation to respond to God in the chat-room conversation. Ask the people questions such as "How are you today?" or "Do you think the Bears will win today? I know the answer already, but you don't have to be omniscient to guess that one."

Then wait for responses from the congregation. Have the person creating the people's side of the conversation type in some of the actual responses people give aloud.

When people appear to be comfortable with the chat-room idea and are responding out loud, steer the conversation toward serious matters. Have God begin to ask questions such as "Do you think we spent enough time together last week?" and "Can you and I set up some time to get together this week?" Ask several such questions, and allow people to respond. Let this conversation last five to 10 minutes before the pastor delivers the message.

Message

Consider using any of the following points in the message:

- God wants us to spend time in conversation with him.
- God cares about us more than we probably will ever realize, as witnessed by what he did for us in sending Jesus to die for us on the cross.
- We can communicate with other people almost instantly through e-mail, chat rooms, and instant messaging. But God is even more accessible to us. All we have to do is think our conversation with him, and he hears it.
- God wants us to listen and look for his responses by reading

and meditating on his Word and by listening for his voice when we're seeking him.

- If we're serious about developing a relationship with God, we'll spend time in conversation with him many times each day.

Communion

Serve Communion in any way that's thought-provoking for your people. During Communion, play soft music, using either live or recorded music. After a few moments, have "instant messages" sporadically pop up on the main screen. Have the first message say, "Thank you for making this time with me a priority." The next should say, "I want you to know I love you." And the last message should say, "This is what I did for you. I sent my only Son."

Worship Response

Turn off the images on the video screens, and dim the lights. Focus a spotlight on a worship leader sitting on a stool in the middle of the congregation. Have the worship leader lead the congregation in singing reflective songs of worship. Here are some suggestions:

- "Pour Out My Heart" by Craig Musseau
- "All I Can Say" by David Crowder
- "Kindness" by Chris Tomlin, Jesse Reeves, and Louie Giglio
- "Let My Words Be Few" by Matt Redman and Beth Redman
- "Lord, You Have My Heart" by Martin Smith
- "Not to Us" by Chris Tomlin and Jesse Reeves
- "O Praise Him" by David Crowder

- "You Are My King" by Billy Foote
- "Hallelujah (Your Love is Amazing)" by Brian Doerksen

Conclusion

Complete the service with a closing challenge to spend more intimate time with God through prayer.

Scripture Index

Topic Index